SPENDING MONEY AND HAVING FUN

Spending Money and
HAVING
FUN

Your Practical Guide to a
Fearless Retirement

Bradly J. Gotto, RICP®

LIONCREST
PUBLISHING

Paperback ISBN: 978-1-5445-3319-3
Ebook ISBN: 978-1-5445-3320-9

To Christy, my high school sweetheart, bride, and rock.

CONTENTS

FOREWORD

Matt Stahl, Co-founder of Fiat

I HAVE KNOWN BRAD FOR OVER FIFTEEN YEARS, AND WE HAVE been through many ups and downs together. There isn't another person in the world I would choose to communicate our company's values and offerings to the world. Brad's ability to meet the client where they are and distill extremely conceptual topics into simple frameworks amazes me. I am truly in awe of this every day. The fact that he truly, deeply cares about the client is something many pay lip service to—however, I witness this firsthand, and it is truly unique.

Brad has summarized our philosophy as a firm and the value we can provide into a neat package that is the book you hold in your hands. This is a book that you can read in a flight and walk away from with some actionable, tactical takeaways. More importantly, you will walk away with a shift in mindset that can serve you for a lifetime…

INTRODUCTION

FEW MOVIES HAVE IMPACTED ME MORE PROFOUNDLY THAN *Free Solo.*

It's a documentary about a rock climber named Alex Honnold. I was on a flight home when I pushed "play" for that feature. The following hour and forty minutes are a blur. I don't recall blinking. Or swallowing. Or getting a Diet Coke from the flight attendant.

Free Solo captured the first successful "clean" climb of Yosemite's El Capitan—a three-thousand-foot ascent of the rock face with no ropes or support. As the final credits rolled and my world came back into focus, I realized I was gripping the armrests so hard, my hands hurt; I was sweating profusely.

The poor lady sitting next to me probably thought I was having a heart attack. And I'm not sure she was wrong.

I can't help it—I'm naturally drawn to stories of men, women, and the proverbial mountains they climb. For climbers, of course, there's really only one Mountain, capital M. That, of course, is Mount Everest, in Nepal—the tallest in the world. Everest stands 29,032 feet high, more than twice the height of the tallest mountain in the US.

Everest makes for a deadly expedition, but that doesn't keep people from taking it on. Each spring, hundreds of climbers show up, ready for the challenge. Many are successful; I can imagine that moment of exhilaration, up where the air is thin. You've made it; your climb is complete.

Yet that's not the end of the story. While the climb is done, the trip is only at the halfway point. There's still the other side of the mountain—the journey down again.

You might think that's no big deal. No one celebrates mountain descents. But as it turns out, the trip down is indeed a big deal. Not only do people die climbing Mount Everest, but they die descending it too! In fact, a quick Google search will point this out very clearly. You see, the record books for who first summited Mount Everest are split. Some give credit to George Mallory, some to Sir Edmund Hillary. Why, you might ask, are opinions divided on this simple issue? Because Hillary didn't just climb Everest. Mallory climbed it, but never made it back down.

This is actually true not only of Everest, but of any demanding mountain expedition. What goes up must come down, and that's where the real danger lies. Most plan carefully for the climb, and the descent is an afterthought, and where many lose their lives.

Why is this true?

For one thing, you're exhausted from climbing by this point. Also, since you've hit your true goal, maybe you're not quite as focused. And more important still, the descent is nothing like the climb; it requires different muscles, different skills.

Believe it or not, I think of retirement planning in similar terms. Your life up to that point is a steady climb. You started out as a young adult, married or single. It was tough going; there was never a lot of money, but there were plenty of expenses. You may have begun to carry debt—like a backpack—and struggled on up the slope.

Still, the years hurried by. Around sixty-five years of age, you found yourself at the highest point. Congratulations! You were ready for retirement. "Now you can take it easy," people told you. It's time to enjoy that pile of money you've accumulated. It's all downhill from here, right?

Here's the truth: This next part of the trip requires a whole different set of skills and "muscles." For so long, you've been geared toward saving, toward accumulating, toward creating security. But now things work differently.

And this is where I think of George Costanza.

George was a character on *Seinfeld*, the highest-rated sitcom of the nineties. He was played so well by Jason Alexander. In one scene, sitting in a diner with his friends Jerry and Elaine, he comes to the realization that, as he put it, "Every decision I've ever made in life is wrong. My life is the complete opposite of everything I have ever wanted." If he wants things to change, it's time to start doing everything in life the exact opposite of how he's always done things.

At that point, Elaine points out to him that a woman has just looked over his way. Jerry and Elaine egg him on; if he's really going to do things the opposite way, he can't chicken out. He has to be bold enough to go talk to her.

George finally walks up to the waitress and says, "My name is George. I'm unemployed. And I live with my parents."

She smiles and says, "I'm Victoria. Hi!"

EVERYTHING OPPOSITE

I would never tell you that, like George, you've made all the wrong decisions. But to move forward in retirement, you're going to have to do things the opposite of what you did to get up there. In your savings years, you may have done things exactly the right way. But now the terrain is different. You've learned to be a good saver, but it's time to figure out how to be a good spender. And that's a lot harder than it sounds!

For one thing, it's unexpected. Unless you've been given very good advice, you didn't see these questions coming. You have your savings, of course. That's your foundation. Then, you might soon be turning on your Social Security payments. Maybe there's also a pension and your own personal savings or "nest egg."

Everyone has their financial variables. But you look at all these moving parts and wonder, "What if it's not enough? How do I know if I'm spending it too quickly, when I don't even know how long I'll be alive?"

Taxes? Trying to understand that subject makes your head spin. It's complexity within complexity. When we retire, we tend to think that particular battle is over, but it's not. Taxes are the greatest issue of all when it comes to financial planning in retirement.

Healthcare is right up there in difficulty, too. In younger years, we never thought about the fact that our medical needs would increase—perhaps even to the point of full-time care—or that this whole category would be so expensive. One major procedure at the hospital, and you may find yourself questioning your financial security.

These are among the challenges you're realizing you'll face. There's no neat, simple formula for solving these complex equations.

This isn't how you envisioned retirement, is it?

It wasn't supposed to be a time of anxiety. You were looking forward to enjoying life comfortably. You may have worked hard for four decades, and those times were filled with the ordinary anxieties that come with work and handling your money. You put in your five days a week and looked to the weekend for relaxation.

Retirement? That was something to look forward to. Surely it wasn't going to feature more stress and anxiety. Nobody sees it like that. You were going to relax and enjoy yourself, and you saved enough money so that you could do just that.

You didn't count on so many unknowns. You didn't realize there would be so many uncertainties about investments, about taxes, about healthcare, and other things.

As for me, I didn't even anticipate dealing with these issues as a career. You could say I stumbled into it, like George Costanza, from the opposite direction.

I was trained to use a different set of career muscles. I was going to be a minister. My passion was (and is) teaching people to enjoy their lives the right way, including in their relationship to money. In the home where I grew up, there wasn't much money. We were a single mom and three kids. I valued money in a different way than others because we never had enough, and it had an impact on how I looked at wealth and our attitudes about it.

I started out working as a youth pastor, but one day, when I was between churches, I discovered a different way to help people—and I knew immediately I'd found my true passion.

I know what some of you are thinking: "You were a youth pastor, and now own a financial advisory practice? That's a whole different book!"

My faith didn't come to me naturally, but from walking a long and winding road. Youth ministry for me was about helping kids find their faith on a less painful, more direct route than mine. Falling into the field of financial advisory scratched the same itch.

I don't teach people how to become rich, but how to spend and enjoy the wealth they possess, rather than getting caught up in the constant pursuit of more. And my faith background is in perfect harmony with my desire to help people be generous.

I may not be in the ministry in the traditional sense, but I'm still following my passion to help people find satisfaction, security, and a sense of purpose for their possessions and their lives ahead.

So by this time, I've worked with thousands of people who sought help with their money. These aren't people who are deeply unhappy with their lives; they're simply coming to the realization that they're not enjoying their money to the fullest.

On the one hand, they have this pile of money they've accumulated through the hard work of half a lifetime. They have the opportunity to do things they enjoy with that wealth. But on the other hand, they're filled with uncertainty about how to use the money, whether and when to use the money, and how far it will go.

There are things they shouldn't fear, and do—and other things they actually *should* worry about and don't, because they're not aware of some of the risks.

We can't provide magic answers to the questions that are out there, but we can help simplify things for you so that you can make the wisest decisions with the best understanding, and that will relieve most or all of the anxiety you'd be feeling.

ARE WE HAVING FUN YET?

Anxiety is the enemy. I believe you should be enjoying yourself to the fullest during this period of your life. You've earned it. You have a certain amount of savings, of Social Security payments, of pensions, or of whatever other sources of money. And you shouldn't be paralyzed by the fears that come from simple uncertainty.

This book is intended to offer you conceptual ideas and strategies, using good common sense, logic, my experience of many years, and a little dash of humor—with one eye on the financial side of things and one on the behavioral side.

Why do we mention the behavioral side? Because at this stage of life, most of us have accumulated a strong collection of life habits. These are powerful. In so many ways, you do certain things because you've always done them that way. But those habits just might be limiting your enjoyment.

If you've been a saver for most of your life, it won't be easy to become a spender. We've all had parents or grandparents who were products of the Great Depression. They saw money in ways that were formed by years of not having any. Their children could spend without thinking about it, but they clung to what had never come easily. I've been there myself, and I know how that feels.

Habits are powerful. So we'll look not just at money itself but the behavioral issues that affect the way we see it and use it. This will be a topic in the first chapter of the book.

We'll work from the foundational idea that money isn't an end in itself but merely something that exists for the purpose of using it. If its mere existence causes us stress and anxiety, we need to know why, and we need to change that. Because the truth is, we all want to be enjoying ourselves.

As a matter of fact, at my firm, we sometimes describe our mission as that of helping people learn how to party! There's nothing more satisfying than seeing someone liberated from fear and anxiety, free to enjoy that trip to Europe, or that new wing on their home they always wanted, or simply the freedom to give generously to causes they care deeply about. They may come to us worried, but we believe we can help them on the road to the fun and pleasure they should be enjoying.

I should also mention what this book will *not* do. We won't be digging deeply into the weeds of economic theory and the fine details of finance. We won't try to disentangle all the strands of the current tax laws or offer you a detailed financial handbook.

The fact is, it would be impossible to write such a book effectively because there are no boilerplate answers to these questions. The proper strategies are different for everyone, and so many aspects of money—taxes and investments, for example—are fluid anyway.

One piece of advice we'll be giving you is this: don't just do what worked for your neighbor or your brother-in-law. They are not you; their details won't match yours. When you set out to descend the mountain, you need a guide who understands you, your situation, your unique desires, and the strategies that would work most effectively for you, moving forward.

So no, we won't get too complex or too financially detailed in this book. To be honest, that would be boring anyway. If there's anything in the world I don't like, it's boring an audience.

What we *will* do is look at your major areas of concern, so that you'll be able to see each one clearly. And we'll look at the best overall strategies and concepts for those areas. Just understanding the landscape will remove a lot of anxiety in itself. And with the right "mountain guide," you'll be prepared to move ahead safely.

The main idea is that it's time to enjoy life. Let's figure out just what kinds of obstacles are ahead, and how to deal with them, so you can get this party started.

CHAPTER 1

A NEW MINDSET

LIKE ALL GOOD ADVISORS, AT MY FIRM WE FIND OUT ALL WE can about our clients before we give advice. Each one has a different life, different resources, and different goals. So we invite people to come to the office and get acquainted, over the course of two or three visits.

I was in my second visit with a new client who'd come to us through our retirement tax workshop. Let's call him Ed. He brought his wife for the visit, so they could explore together what our firm had to offer. In a second visit like this one, we begin to offer some recommendations based on what we've learned. But we're still asking questions: What do you want to do with these next few years? What are your dreams? Is there something you've always wanted to do?

Ed was quick to answer that last question: "Yes, I've always dreamed of visiting Normandy."

He was talking about D-Day, of course. On June 6, 1944, Allied troops landed on the Normandy beaches in France, and began the conquest of Europe that would help end the Second World War.

"I had family members there," Ed told me. "I've read books about it. I've watched TV documentaries. I'd just love to walk on those beaches for myself, and relive that amazing beach landing."

As he described his dream, I listened closely—but I was also doing some quick calculations on my cell phone's calculator.

Ed had told me earlier that he had a decent position in Ford stock. Ford had just recently stopped paying a dividend, and he was a bit concerned about that lost income stream. He didn't state it outright, but I could tell he wasn't confident about his finances, about the stability of the markets and economy—and on top of this, he had Parkinson's and didn't know how long he'd be capable of traveling. So even in retirement, he lacked the confidence to say yes to the one trip he most wanted to make.

I looked down at my calculations and said, "Well, based on the amount of money you're pulling out of your portfolio to live on each month, consider this. Imagine you take all your money out of the markets, so there's no more risk there.

"Then, let's say we take all the money you have, and put it in a coffee can and bury it in your backyard."

I had his full attention by this time.

"At that point, you'd just keep going to that coffee can and pulling out the same amount of money every month, right?" I paused and glanced at my calculator. "Ed, did you know your money would last for two hundred years, all by itself, doing nothing but sitting there in the coffee can?"

He was shocked. Ed's wife had sat quietly, but now she smiled and gave her husband that look that said, "I told you so."

"You should book your flight without waiting any longer," I said. "There's no reason you shouldn't visit Normandy. I know you're worried about running out of money, but that's a game you've already won!"

Ed took a deep breath as I continued, "You're all set, unless your cost of living suddenly rockets. And I'm going to make a guess because I've gotten to know you two, that a drastic change like that is highly unlikely. You can go to Normandy without a care in the world. And if you want, you can go there again next year and the year after that."

Ed's world was rocked. It was as if he'd won the Publisher's Clearing House Sweepstakes months ago, but nobody told him. He just hadn't realized what he had and what it meant.

Sometimes, when you've won the game, it's okay to take a victory lap. But you won't know you've won unless you understand how to read the scoreboard. That's what I love helping our clients do. As a matter of fact, we have the long-term goal of having a travel agent on-site, so I can walk the Eds of the future down the hall and help them fulfill their dreams then and there.

BOUNDARIES

Ed is typical of hundreds of people I've met, who have come to that point in their journey. It can be a frightening point, and all the worry comes from a simple fear of the unknown.

Of the many questions surrounding retirement age, the greatest of all is, "How much time are we talking about?" No one can answer that question. We simply can't know how much time is allotted for us. For the most part, that's a good thing. We'd rather not be watching the clock tick down with any precision.

But our lack of knowledge also creates stress and uncertainty. We can know how much money we have, to the penny—even if our investments fluctuate. We can have a pretty good idea of how much it costs to live each day, week, and month. But the X-factor is time remaining. If I have a million dollars, do I divide that by five years, or thirty years—or more?

Longevity is a huge question, and that's why we've devoted the sixth chapter of this book to it.

There's another source of anxiety, and thankfully, it comes with solutions. Many people have never set up boundaries for themselves. Ed didn't know where his boundaries were—what he could or could not do. How much money could he spend on a vacation? He had the pile of money he and his wife had accumulated, but he had no idea what it would pay for and for how long. He'd never realized those questions would present themselves.

Around my office, we often say there's no freedom without boundaries. That may seem like a contradiction in terms because we think of freedom as the removal of restrictions. But imagine taking a trip to the beach. The ocean and the sand are beautiful, and you decide you'd like to take a dip in the water.

But you've heard vague rumors of sharks. Can you swim safely here? Can you even *enjoy* swimming, if there's the smallest chance these are shark-infested waters? I couldn't! The uncertainty would keep me on dry land.

But then the beach patrol comes along and sets up a series of buoys. They're bright, they're set in place, and they're easy to see. You're told that within those buoys, there's zero chance of sharks.

That changes your mindset, right? Now you have the freedom to have a relaxing swim in the ocean—because boundaries have been established.

A good financial advisor scopes out the shore, checks for sharks, and sets up visible buoys that offer safe limits, with money rather than water. The coffee can illustration, for Ed, was a way of understanding the water was safe for as far as his eyes could see—two hundred years into the future, actually. He simply hadn't realized it, because he had never looked for boundaries. Now he could swim to his heart's content.

Our need for boundaries, and the freedom they give us, points to another surprising element of planning our future. Our clients come to us with ideas of talking about cash, investments, and funds. Surely financial planning is done in financial terms, right?

Sure it is, but we also need to have conversations about *thinking*, about behavior. In the end, these are the factors that make the difference.

It's not just about how many dollars we can spend, and when we should spend them. What we need most to understand is *why* we spend. Believe it or not, there's an entire field of study on this topic, called *behavioral finance*.

For example: What do you feel when you spend money? Is it pleasurable? Uncomfortable? Where does your approach to spending come from?

THINKING ABOUT THINKING

We handle money as we do everything: individually. No two people see and use their finances in exactly the same way. A man born and raised and pampered in a wealthy home would have a certain attitude about spending. Your parents or grandparents—products of the Great Depression—would likely have a very different approach.

We bear the imprint of how we're raised and what happens in our lives. We develop behavior patterns in every part of life, including how we spend and how we save.

The stock market, by the way, is no different. It has certain behaviors, certain predictable patterns. We talk about a market being "bullish," being "in a frenzy," or being "skittish"—these are all attitudes markets show because markets are made of people. The best investors, of course, closely study that aspect of the market. Once they understand the psychology, they can maneuver successfully in it.

But let's focus on ourselves and our own attitudes and patterns of behavior. Most people I know would say they're very rational, very logical in how they use their money. They would say they think carefully and objectively about each decision, then act thoughtfully to make the right choice.

But is this always true? Think about the last few times you've spent money, whether large or small sums. You might be surprised at the factors that guided your decisions.

For example, what's your basic attitude toward money? What did your parents teach you and model for you? What life experiences have shifted the way you think about money, or spend it? Teaching, experience, and our basic personality profile have a greater impact than most of us realize.

Are we thinking logically and objectively when we buy the candy bar near the cash register, where it's been deliberately positioned as an "impulse item"? I can only speak for myself. I don't tend to think, "This would be a sensible way to use some of my money at this moment." But I can certainly imagine myself thinking, "I've had a hard day. I need comfort food, and this candy bar looks delicious." My decision was emotion-based rather than logic-based.

That's just an ordinary example, and a harmless one. But isn't the same set of attitudes in operation when we make larger purchasing decisions?

Now you can see why, at firms like ours, we spend plenty of time in conversation with our clients, rather than simply tapping away at our calculators and creating spreadsheets. We consider their lives, goals, and dreams, but we also get to know who they are as people, how they think, and sometimes where they *don't* think.

For example, many people avoid thinking about aging and death because they consider those subjects unpleasant. Tragically, we all know that some people reach the end of life without ever having thought seriously or prepared for the eventuality of it.

To avoid that subject is to fail to question our assumptions and presuppositions. I find that, for some reason, we men seem to assume we'll die before we reach our eighties or nineties. We say things like, "My mom died at such and such an age. That's how it goes in our family."

But are we willing to bet all our finances on that assumption? We need to ask the right questions, even when they're uncomfortable. Learning to think in a new way means learning new habits.

HABITS

One of the greatest obstacles of all is *habit*. As we discussed in the introduction, we're up against years of climbing the mountain; now we need that separate set of muscles, which, in terms of financial planning, means a different mindset. Since we started our careers, maybe four decades ago, we've been saving, always saving. Our minds are almost on autopilot when it comes to that principle. Save for the future! Save some more!

But the future has become *now*. We know that logically, rationally, and consciously. But habits of nearly half a century can be quite difficult to break. Whenever we write a check or pull out a credit card, some impulse within wants us to ride the brake rather than step on the gas. That impulse is so ingrained in us that we're not quite sure how to turn it off.

There's a word scientists use: *homeostasis*. It occurs in nature, including in the human personality. We like balance, and we instinctively move back toward it when something changes. How many people have you heard say, "I hate change"? Stress is actually defined as the body's reaction to some perceived change.

It's like the thermostat in your house. It's set at a certain point for your comfort, and the system adjusts one way or the other to maintain that temperature. Ludvig Sunstrom's book *Breaking Out of Homeostasis* makes the point that this urge toward balance is in our DNA. It's actually an energy conservation device, and a helpful one. Change uses energy.

But homeostasis also keeps us from growing and changing. And because of it, we can't totally trust our mind or body, which lean toward not rocking the boat rather than taking the step that might actually be beneficial.

Sunstrom says that change should happen gradually because we need time to adapt. So as you move from saving mode to spending mode, you need to realize you can't trust those old instincts. They're remnants of a different era. It's time to learn a new way of thinking. In your home, you'll adjust the thermostat as you move into a new season. You'll use the heater rather than the air conditioning. In the same way, you're in a new season of life. It's time to make that adjustment.

Here's an example. Let's say you have a million dollars or more in assets, and the mortgage on your house is paid off. The kids are out of the house and now building their own careers and families. There are no immediate, pressing financial needs—at least for the moment. And you and your spouse have been given clean bills of health on your recent physicals. It's all good.

Now you come across a chance to make a trip around the world with another couple, or invest in a vacation home, or make some home improvements you've talked about for years. How do you feel about spending on such things? You know the money is there, you know you can afford it, but it just doesn't feel right?

Give it a little more thought. Adjust your mental thermostat.

I haven't met anyone yet who wants to be the richest individual in the cemetery. At the end of the day, you have two choices of what to do with your money: you can spend it or you can give it to someone else to spend, such as your children or perhaps a cause you support. We'll talk more about the giving aspect of things later in this book. But when we look at the binary choice, most people I talk to decide they're looking for the right balance between spending for their own pleasure, giving to good causes, and leaving something for their children or grandchildren.

That's why it's so important to understand your feelings about money. Those feelings are different for all of us, based on some of the factors I've mentioned—upbringing, experience, personality type. For some people, money means power or status; for others, security; and for others, opportunity. What does it mean to you? What would you like it to mean for your future?

I've found James Clear's book, *Atomic Habits: An Easy & Proven Way to Build Good Habits & Break Bad Ones*, helpful for myself and my clients. Clear says that just as matter is composed of the tiniest units, known as atoms, our lives are built on tiny units known as habits. And just as atoms hold fantastic power disproportionate to their size, habits are powerful in taking us where we want to go in life—or stopping us from getting there. All our habits, taken together, are the system by which we live our lives. Yet most of them aren't thoughtfully adopted, and a great many are harmful.

We all want to change for the better. The desire for it isn't the problem; having the wrong system for it is. Clear's book shows how tiny changes that seem small and trivial at first will bear tremendous results in the future. It's like the "butterfly effect"—tiny changes now cause ripple effects that echo into the years to come. We simply need to make those tiny changes, then live by them consistently.

But aren't certain things unchangeable? Take the subject of tax, for example. Most people think it is what it is when it comes to those payments. But they're wrong. Our next chapter on taxes shows why.

CHAPTER 2

THE TAX QUESTION

THE IDEA OF INCOME TAX IS NOTHING NEW. THERE ARE TAX codes in the oldest records of ancient Egypt, from the dawn of civilization. Five minutes after someone invented and sold the first wheel, another guy probably invented a way to tax it.

But for those of us who are Americans, the process actually hasn't been around too long. It wasn't until 1861 that Abraham Lincoln instituted the first American income tax. The Civil War was starting, and it was clearly going to stress the US Treasury. Somebody out there had to generate a way to pay for uniforms, weapons, and soldiers.

In retrospect, perhaps we should be glad the new taxing regulations didn't start a whole other war. Taxes are about as popular as root canals. We Americans are independent-minded; we tend to be grumpy about sharing our hard-earned income with politicians.

Yet those taxes did help us build a great nation. They got us through two world wars and continue to help us defend our shores from attack. And they've built interstate highways, national parks, and other good things.

"But it's too much!" you might say, and I hear you. I share your feelings about April 15. But taxes—federal, state, and local—are here to stay. As a matter of fact, federal income tax has been worse in the past—much worse.

Let's look at history again. From 1915 to 1918, as the US prepared for and then entered the First World War, the highest marginal rate leapt from 7 percent to 77 percent! When the troops came home, it decreased, ever so slightly, to 73 percent.

Over the years, the top marginal rate worked its way all the way down to the twenties, then spiked again during the Great Depression. Once again, Uncle Sam was hard up for cash.

By 1945, while Americans celebrated the end of World War II, the top rate was a staggering 94 percent. That rate fluctuated between the seventies and nineties for decades. When Ronald Reagan entered office in 1981, he ultimately brought the figure down to 50 percent—a figure Congress promised was here to stay. As we all know, they were wrong. It lasted all of three years.

You may be aware that the top marginal rate as I write this chapter is 37 percent. Yes, it's still "too much," according to popular opinion. We'd love to lower it even more. But the fact is, we're paying lower taxes by percentage than we have since 1931. A relatively lower rate gives us far greater opportunities to save and invest.

What *has* increased is the complexity of the tax code. The laws can be confusing and even painful, if we're not careful. In our tax code, there's a whole section that most of us have never read, never heard much about, and never planned for, simply because we haven't had to. This is the part of the tax code that applies specifically to retirees.

Some people even get the notion that once they enter retirement, tax is a problem of the past. They identify taxes with earnings, and the earning years are past. But it's not that simple: as we retire, income continues, and taxes follow. There are tax implications in all the ways you might handle your money. And it can become complicated. We hear a lot of talk about simplifying the tax code, but here we are.

Most of us just take our taxes, and how we pay them, for granted, but try and imagine this. You walk into a restaurant, the waitstaff shows you a menu, and you begin to order various courses. There are lots of variations on how dishes can be served and how much they cost. At the end of the meal, you ask for the bill, but the waiter tells you, "That's up to you. We have definite fees, but the customers must figure them out for themselves. And please make sure you get it right. Penalties can be assessed."

Not only that, but if you're married, you and your spouse get separate checks—or rather, must figure out separate bills. You might have shared a basket of bread and a dessert, but that has to be sorted out for each of you. This is how our tax system works. The 1040 form is an invoice from the IRS, but you fill in all the items, and the total is "you tell me!" It's called a "voluntary tax system," but voluntary doesn't mean we decide whether to pay. It means we volunteer all the figuring.

Our tax code is a bit more complex than a restaurant's menu, too, and our tax bill intersects with all the other topics we discuss in this book. Let's keep it simple for now, however. We'll limit our focus to some of the more crucial issues about taxes during retirement.

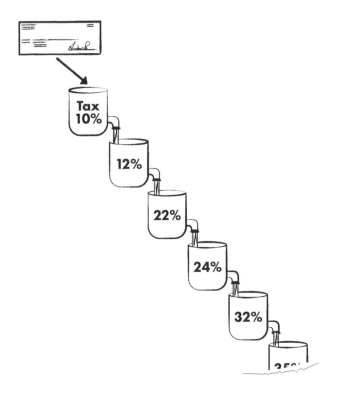

The most basic idea we need to understand is that your tax liability is a moving target. That is, it changes in real time based on your income.

Imagine you've placed a bucket in your home at the beginning of a new year. You plan to drop all your income into it as it comes in the door, for tax purposes. The first bucket is actually marked with a big zero because your first earnings won't require any tax payments. Isn't that nice? Up to a certain amount of income, you'll pay zero taxes.

Our tax code is set up with a standard deduction, which is really just a fancy way of saying you can make a certain amount of money without paying taxes. The limit depends upon whether you're married or single, but we all have that standard deduction. The first bucket after zero happens to be 10 percent, as I write. But I don't use a lot of numbers because they can change. Our lawmakers do a great deal of tinkering with the tax code, you might have noticed. You can Google it if you're curious.

After you reach that number, you stop using the zero bucket, and move to a new one you now place right beside it. Your next earnings—again up to a certain limit—will require a certain percentage of taxes. You're part of the tax code now, and you owe the government for any moneys that come in the door. When you reach that limit, you move to a third bucket, which shows a higher percentage. Through the year, depending on how much wealth you accumulate, you will pay taxes not for your total but for which bucket you were using at the time.

Let's stop and realize the implications of that simple process, because many people don't understand that it works that way. They think, "I make x dollars a year, so I'm liable for this amount of tax." But it really depends upon when you received how much of that. If you were handed a check on December 31 for a year's pay, you're liable for that full amount. But in the real world, your first earnings aren't taxable; your earnings up to a certain point are less taxable; and so it goes, through seven buckets.

Another mental image I use to picture this process is one of those decorative fountains we see. The water comes out way up top and flows into a basin just below it. As that basin fills, it overflows into a larger one below that, and then to a still larger one. You get the picture. Your taxes flow like that water, into ever larger basins (or buckets) of tax liability.

This means the timing of your payments is important. The first bucket is always zero, the next is 10 percent for now, and the highest is currently 37 percent—but these numbers are always subject to change. As Will Rogers said, "The only difference between death and taxes is that death doesn't get worse every time congress meets."

A lot of things don't change from working years to retirement—money comes in, tax goes out based on income level. What has changed is that you no longer have a steady paycheck coming in the door through a W2 job, or perhaps money you pay to yourself through a personal business.

But that's replaced by income from other sources. You have a Social Security payment, and it's taxable within its own set of rules. We discuss some of these in our Social Security chapter. You may also be fortunate enough to have a pension check that was provided from past employment, or in the form of a fund you set up. Then you might also be pulling money from retirement accounts you've been saving for four decades. Finally, there's your "pile of money," as I call it. Your money might have three different tax statuses because some could be classified as pre-tax money, or after-tax money, or even tax-free money.

In retirement, then, you figure a budget for how much you need coming in your door from all these sources. This will be your new income, and you have to figure out where it will come from, among the sources we've named. There can be a lot of complications because the various streams of money will interact in different ways with that tax bill the IRS wants you to work up. Because of the tax implications, money isn't simply money. Some kinds of money are more expensive than others—and some are bargains!

I say often, "The amount of income you need to live on in retirement does not determine your tax bill. Where your income comes from will ultimately determine your tax bill."

Let's look at some examples.

SOCIAL SECURITY

This topic has its own chapter, but we want to discuss here some basic principles of how it interacts with your tax bill. We all spend years paying into the Social Security program, and naturally, we look forward to the day it begins paying us back.

Social Security is based on your provisional income. That's the sum of wages, taxable and nontaxable interest, taxable income, plus 50 percent of your annual Social Security benefit. Your marital status also has an effect on this number. What's important for now is to understand that it's possible to get your Social Security payments tax-free. And it's all based upon provisional income.

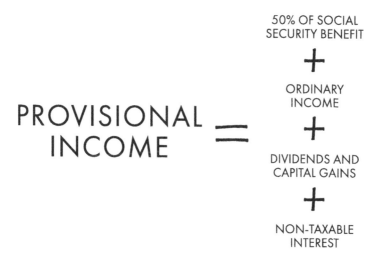

Basically, figure your provisional income based upon the numbers above (or ask your accountant to do so). Currently, if the four numbers add up to less than $32,000, then your Social Security is tax-free. Keep in mind that any numbers or rates we mention here are subject to change.

At Fiat Wealth Management, we work with families who live on six-figure incomes a year in retirement, and they pay no taxes on their Social Security. Based on the principles I've described, that may seem impossible. If you're over the current $32,000 figure I've mentioned, normally you would start paying taxes on your social security benefit, based on a sliding scale as those numbers climb.

But some of the income they're living on is actually tax-free. And all that matters for provisional income is what actually appears on the 1040—the taxable money. So it's possible your provisional income figure could be $30,000, even though you have another $70,000 that doesn't show up because the government allows that money to be tax-free. I like to refer to this money as "off-the-grid money."

It's one of many reasons, needless to say, you need to make a strong plan in advance. Tax-free Social Security is a wonderful thing, but it doesn't happen by itself. It all depends upon those various sources of money that make up your retirement income.

REQUIRED MINIMUM DISTRIBUTIONS

As we think again about the "buckets" where we place our money, we find that most of our families saved their money in a pre-tax bucket. That is, there are ways to keep your money in a tax-deferred state for a certain period of time. You might have been paying into an employer-sponsored plan like a 401(k), 403(b), or others. Or, you have a Traditional IRA (Individual Retirement Account).

Up to now, all of that was tax-deferred—but at a certain time, the IRS

Age	Distribution Period
72	27.4
73	26.5
.	.
.	.
.	.
82	18.5
83	17.7

wants to be paid. Taxes can no longer be deferred. The IRS gives you a schedule of your process of paying taxes on everything you've had in the pre-tax bucket. The IRS keeps a table to show you how much to pay each year, and the numbers seem to be highly random—25.6 percent or 26.7 percent. Who knows how they come up with these? (I do know, but I told you I would keep this book fun and light!) Those are called required minimum distributions. Each RMD year, currently after age 72, you'll look at your total pre-tax assets (IRA, 401(k), and the like), divide it by the number that corresponds to their table, and that's the amount that will immediately be taxable.

Many families are moving happily through retirement, and perhaps seven or more years in, and they've let that RMD age sneak up on them. The payments can be large, painful, and completely unplanned-for—just another of the complexities so many people never see coming, because frankly, they haven't spent much time thinking about retirement income.

Not long ago, the magic age was 70 and six months; then it was changed to 72, and as I write this book, there are discussions of changing it again! So keep in mind that almost nothing in the tax code is carved in stone. All these requirements can change. The number actually could be moved to 75, but I predict one thing never changing: the IRS will want to settle up with us on that pre-tax money. The biggest mistake we see people make is to wait for that time to come before making plans because then, of course, they've lost the power to control what happens.

Here's an important way to think about it. Currently from the age of 59.5, the pre-tax money in your IRA or 401(k) became accessible to you without penalty. You could draw on it at your leisure. Before and after that, the IRS would come after you for drawing on that money. During RMD years, a missed payment carries a 50 percent penalty. None of us want that.

But if you subtract 59.5 from 72, you come up with 12.5 years. That's a good bit of time to control that money and maximize its position for the time when those payments will come due.

THE SECRET OF TIMING

The largest debt most of our families bring with them is not a mortgage. Some of them have paid off their mortgages, of course, but even if they have one, that's not the largest debt before them. The largest is the pre-tax money they've been accumulating. As we've seen, taxes are going to come due on Social Security, on pensions, and on all the other funds we've been able to shield up to now. And often, people don't realize what the size of that bill will be, or how it will be collected.

The most important task, then, is figuring out the least expensive way to pay off that debt. In a way, it's as if you've taken out a second mortgage on your home. You know a bill is coming due, and you want to figure out whether it is best to make a minimum payment, or to pay it all off ahead of time.

But the IRS debt must be treated differently. For one thing, many people have a misperception in how they see their pre-tax money. They think of it as "their money," and that's not entirely true. Some of it's theirs; some of it's debt. That's just part of the arrangement. Also, there isn't a predetermined rate to be paid, as there is with a mortgage. Nor is there a predetermined time for paying, as in a 30-year mortgage, because this is actually a debt you could pass on to your kids.

You could pay it in your lifetime, as all of us would want, or you could leave the debt for others to pay—but one way or another, it has to be paid.

It's worth noting here that passing that debt on to your kids, grandkids, or other family members has the potential of increasing the debt. In other words, it could be more expensive to leave it for them than to pay it yourself—an outcome few of us would desire.

Let's keep in mind our historical context, as introduced at the beginning of the chapter. These are actually good times for us in terms of tax rates. In the past, we've had to pay a higher percentage. But times are not so wonderful in terms of our national debt. The debt-to-income ratio in our country is as high as it's ever been. Add to that the fact that our government has only two ways to raise more money: they can print more, or they can charge you higher prices, by raising taxes.

Because of these factors, wisdom dictates that the present is likely to offer you a lower bill than later. Taxes could increase; it's probably just a matter of time. Therefore, it makes sense to create a payment plan now, and find the best schedule and best procedures for paying down the debt of pre-tax income that retirement will bring. You may, for example, choose to take out money earlier than you expected and pay the taxes on it now rather than later.

Sometimes we explain that concept and receive pushback: "Why would I take money from my 401k or my IRA when I don't need it yet? I budgeted based on what I'm going to spend." And our response is that taking it out and spending it are two different things. You don't have to spend it; you're simply saving yourself money later by paying lower taxes now.

Your plan will make concepts of that type clear and sensible. And the plan shouldn't be for next year, or even the next five years; it should look ahead to 10 years, 20, or even 30 years in the future. We know that we're living longer than our parents and grandparents. We know that we don't have any understanding of what the future holds in economic terms. Armed with a solid plan, you can gain control over the largest expense you're likely to have in retirement.

This subject always brings me back to that philosophy that there's no freedom without boundaries. You create intelligent boundaries by putting together a plan for the future and for your money. You reduce surprises, hidden expenses sneaking up, and taxes you never even realized you were liable for. And you may even remove some liabilities, such as the Social Security tax, simply through diligent planning.

Taxes are as old as humanity, and as inevitable as tomorrow's sunrise. They don't stop when you stop working; they actually become more complicated. Albert Einstein, who developed the theory of relativity, said, "The hardest thing in the world to understand is the income tax." If he struggled with it, the rest of us probably need a little help, too—along with a sound plan and a smart team.

CHAPTER 3

WIDOW OR WIDOWER?

SEVENTY YEARS IS A LONG TIME TO BE MARRIED. WHEN WE HEAR about a couple reaching that milestone, we can't help but admire them.

I always have to do the math. Seventy years of marriage works out to 25,567 days together on this planet. That's a lot of sunsets, a lot of rainy and sunny days, a lot of memories—it's a lot, period.

On the other side of this coin, what are the chances that the husband and wife die naturally on the same day?

The DeLaigles did that on a Friday in 2019. Herbert was 94, and Marilyn was 88. They'd been married 70 years, utterly devoted to one another. On the day they met, she was a waitress at the diner, and he was an admiring customer.

He died at 2:20 a.m. She died at 2:20 p.m., precisely 12 hours later.

That's a story that appeals to most of us, because those of us with happy marriages hate the thought of being left alone. Leaving together seems perfect.

At the other extreme there's Walter Breuning who, at the time of his death in 2011, was the world's oldest living man. He outlived his first wife by 54 years—then outlived his second wife by another 36 years.

I would venture to guess that most of us would rather follow the lead of the DeLaigles. Yet what are the chances that actually happens? These couples made the news because their stories were unique. The rest of us are likely to die more than a day, but less than 54 years, from the death of our spouse.

None of us knows when or how, and we can all agree that's for the best.

Are you a bit uncomfortable with this subject? No one enjoys discussing the loss of a soulmate, or death in general. But urgent questions are connected here; it's unwise to avoid them. We may not like to think about automobile accidents, but we take care to buckle our seat belts and renew our insurance policies.

The question of surviving or predeceasing a spouse is similar; we hope for the best and prepare for the worst. Then again, you may be unmarried. Does this chapter apply to you?

Yes, I think so. Your personal situation may not be affected, but I'm sure you know and care about a few married couples. And we'll be discussing one of the most egregious errors people make in their retirement planning process. From the perspectives of income, tax, and estate, there are significant dangers in ignoring the reality that one of us will outlive the other. So if you're single, keep reading. These facts will help you have a good talk with some of your friends who may be widows or widowers.

There are three significant financial aspects of losing a spouse. There's an income effect, a tax effect, and finally, an estate effect. As I've suggested previously, many of the subjects in this book overlap and impact each other. For example, in the previous chapter, we discussed taxes as a basic issue—and taxes come into play for widows and widowers. Social Security is another example, as we'll soon see.

Good planning is a hedge against big problems in this and every case. In this chapter, we'll take on each one of these questions.

INCOME: SOCIAL SECURITY

We're always shocked to lose a good friend or family member "before their time." When exactly is "their time"? We figure it's sometime in their seventies or eighties. But as we all know, a spouse may die significantly earlier, long before his or her Social Security period begins. In today's world, of course, it's far more likely to have two married partners who have earned Social Security benefits than, say, seventy years ago, when there were fewer women in the workforce. So, how does this affect a couple when one partner dies? There are various scenarios, and it's important to know what they are.

One spouse may have begun accepting payments, the other not. As a surviving spouse, you still have access to the benefit of the deceased, even if you haven't yet filed—a fact many people don't understand. This could make a huge difference in couples with a large discrepancy in income and the associated Social Security contributions and relevant benefits because Social Security is based on how much you contributed. For example, if one was a banker and the other a music teacher, there might be a large difference in the size of their benefits because they earned and contributed different amounts over the course of their working years.

Or, both may have initiated their Social Security payments. At the death of the first spouse, the survivor receives the larger of the two payments—regardless of who earned that payment. He or she can collect the late spouse's full benefit if the survivor has reached full retirement age. (Again, the amount is lower if the deceased spouse claimed benefits before reaching full retirement age.) To be clear, there is a lot of nuance here. As a reminder, this book does not serve as an exhaustive manual, but to introduce the concepts and guiding principles—a point I will most likely repeat in coming chapters.

That's the good news. On the other hand, it's still true that only one check will now arrive in the mail. While it will be the larger of the two checks, that still makes for a significant loss of income for the survivor, and one that very few people realize is coming. This could be a loss of nearly half the Social Security income that the couple had come to expect.

Keep in mind that expenses will *not* be cut in half. If there's a mortgage payment, it remains the same. A car payment remains due each month. Utilities and other bills might change slightly, but won't be cut in half. The loss of one Social Security payment can create financial problems that were never anticipated. The surviving spouse may think, "My income just shrunk. I have to start living more cheaply."

But it's my experience that these people haven't counted at all on doing that. If the two of them were living on $80,000 annually, that's still the amount the survivor desires to maintain their lifestyle. This fact flies in the face of my formal education. I was taught that the surviving spouse would need/want around 75 percent of the income at the death of the first spouse. Practically, I have yet to see that play out.

In the wake of losing a soulmate, we're likely to think, "I've just lost the love of my life. I have no desire to talk about money." Of course! The last thing we want to be doing in such a dark time is running a spreadsheet or going over a checkbook. We want a seamless and gentle transition to whatever lies ahead. This gentle transition never involves a pay cut.

This is why we need to be thinking ahead, making retirement and later-life plans sooner rather than later. That begins with a firm understanding that our income is going to take a hit when one of our two Social Security checks stops arriving.

But there are other income questions.

INCOME: PENSIONS AND ANNUITIES

Is your family fortunate enough to have a pension? If so, does it contain a survivor benefit? That's the next question.

A pension plan is another fund by which employers—corporate, military, government—help us store away funds for retirement. Survivor benefits help to set our minds at ease because we know there will be at least some financial assistance for the spouse who outlives us.

Let's say one spouse worked for many years for a firm, and of course, more and more, was likely to have worked at a number of different companies during the life of the career. This worker may have had a number of different plans. The first question is, did he or she receive one pension or more? The second is, did they elect a survivor option in any of these? The third is, if so, at what rate? Was it 25 percent? Fifty percent? Seventy-five or more?

You need to know exactly what's been set up. If you're reading this, you're enrolled in a pension plan, and you haven't elected survivor benefits, I'd strongly recommend doing a simple cost/benefit analysis. In picking up that benefit for your surviving spouse, you're actually buying life insurance—except instead of the survivor receiving the benefit in a lump sum, it comes in an income stream for the rest of that person's life, at whatever level you've elected to lock in. That might be 25, 50, 75, or 100 percent continuity in income.

Your plan may also include annuities, which are fixed sums paid on a regular basis over time. If you have annuities, they'd be either single or joint life, depending on your plans for the future. This is oversimplified for our purposes in this book, but the concept of choosing how the income comes to your family, and the guarantees it does or does not have, are imperative to the decision-making for your family.

As you look to the future, you need to know the difference between the income you have coming in the door each month as a family, and what it might be when one of you "ends your retirement." (Stay with me here, I'm getting sick of using the word death.) Once you know what that number is, you can bridge the gap through annuities, which can come from a lot of different sources—savings accounts, investments, or life insurance plans, for example. You could even build an investment portfolio that pays dividend income.

The key here is worth repeating: simply knowing what's already there. What pensions and annuities already exist in your name and/or your spouse's name? Simply having that information at your fingertips will encourage you to begin creating a financial plan certain to decrease your anxiety level and give you confidence that your spouse is well-covered for the remainder of their life.

TAXES

After the last chapter, did you think we had this topic covered? Once again, we can run, but we cannot hide! Taxes are an inevitable part of all our discussions. They reach into virtually every crevice of your life. It's almost like the IRS designed it that way! They follow money like smoke follows fire. And it seems as if there are always new tax problems.

For example, the widow or widower is suddenly single. That's enough of a life adjustment in and of itself. But the federal tax adjustment is pretty jarring, too.

Just glance at the tax brackets for someone who's married and then for a single filer. It's obvious that single people, including widows and widowers, lose some tax advantages. I could show a multitude of examples from real life to make my point. Even with the same amount of income each month, after good planning, the tax code now approaches the survivor as a single filer. Typically, this means a dramatic uptick in the effective tax rate. Bottom line, assuming the same amount of income, deductions, etc., it's cheaper from a tax perspective to be married.

Let's think about the scenario of a couple filing a joint return. Both have Social Security payments. The husband has a pension and receives quarterly IRA distributions. And please, don't say his wife "didn't work." She had the hardest job: staying home and raising the kids.

The total working income for the couple was $96,000, or $8,000 per month.

In retirement, they look to maintain the same budget of $8,000 per month because that's the life they've built together. The good news is they've accumulated plenty of money; no problem there. They look over their continuing income, their pensions, their annuities, and everything looks good on that front.

At the time I write this book (as we know, Congress has an affinity for change), the effective tax rate on their 1040 has been about 7.77 percent—until the husband passes away. Now everything *but* the income changes.

His widow meets with her CPA, her broker, and other professionals. She's grieving and she finds "money talk" distasteful. But she tells the advisors she still requires the budget she's had, which is $8,000 per month. She's keeping the house, life is no less expensive, and she doesn't have the mindset for extensive life changes right now anyway.

Well, the money is still coming in. But now she ends up with a larger tax bill. In fact, it almost doubles to an effective rate of 14.2 percent. This is simply because she's filing single. This is something my industry calls the "Widow's Tax." (It's an "inside baseball" kind of thing.)

It doesn't matter who died first, or any such questions. She's looking at an 82.75 percent tax increase (the difference between

7.77 and 14.2). Now she definitely has to make thousands of dollars' worth of adjustments she never considered.

I've seen this scenario more than once, and it happens when there's a lack of preparation, of looking to the future and seeking good advice. Remember that up to retirement, your money has largely been in a pre-tax bucket. In the last chapter, we talked about the best time to pay a tax bill. The answer is, when it's "on sale"—that is, when the rate is at its lowest.

There's a sale for a brief period right now because of the 2017 tax law, but that's not all. There's what amounts to another one if you're married—and only while you're married—because there are exemptions and deductions that won't be available to a single individual.

Think about the future. If you're going to have $80,000 or $100,000 as income for living, take care of your tax situation as a married person, not as a single filer. It's a cheaper bill.

In building out your income continuity plan, whether on your own or with the help of an advisor, you have to keep an eye on tax liability. It's yet another angle many people fail to anticipate. If you think about a widow living twenty years longer than her husband, without remarrying—something fairly common these days—that's a long time to be filing at a significantly higher rate.

Once you understand that the IRS will be taking a larger bite, it becomes clear you need to rethink whatever number you expect as a living expense. When most people talk about having $100,000 of income in retirement, they really mean $100,000 to spend. In the scenario above, the income wasn't a problem, but the tax spike meant she needed more income than before, simply because Uncle Sam's bill went up.

Can your portfolio handle that? Better yet, do you want it to, even if it can? Have you planned around the current tax code, and are you taking advantage of the married filing joint rates you enjoy today?

ESTATE ISSUES

As we've seen, there are income and then tax issues to consider as we look to the possibility of losing a spouse. On top of these, it's critical to have the legal documents in place to make sure there's a smooth transition of asset transfer to the surviving spouse. Obviously, the time to make those plans is while both of you are still alive, married, and capable of making smart financial adjustments with wise guidance.

Here's a disclaimer: I'm not an estate planning attorney. When it comes to the specifics of this area, you'll want to talk to someone who has that license. But I do know that too many people assume that estate inheritance is somehow an automatic process—that if one dies, everything very simply passes to the spouse.

In some cases, it might well work out that way. But you'll want to check that out for yourself, correct? Surely you wouldn't leave it to chance.

The other issue I'd encourage a couple to look at, if they have a significant estate, is their state's estate tax law. It may be that the exemption you receive before you have to start paying state estate taxes, or "death taxes" as they're known on the street, is on a per-person basis, rather than a marriage basis.

In my state, Minnesota, there's a $3 million per person exemption. This, of course, is subject to change, but let's look at it conceptually, regardless of where the dollar amount goes. Let's take the example of a couple with a $5 million estate. All the assets are in his name, not hers. She passes away, and the exemption goes to waste as a result. Her name was unattached, so there's no exemption to claim.

But in the husband's case, with all the assets in his name, there's still only a $3 million exemption. The bill for the difference could have been avoided if the couple had titled things appropriately, or had applicable trust documents, so as to work around the state's exemption number.

Quite often, nothing more than the simple titling of an account, a beneficiary designation, or perhaps the more complex issues of having the proper legal documents in place would allow a couple to ensure continuity of income, as well as maximizing the passing of assets without taxes.

As you can see, it's not as simple as "If I die, my spouse gets everything." Estate planning, like everything else, I'm afraid, can take on some complexities, depending upon your actual situation. For widows and widowers, I would say income is the most important issue, particularly with regard to Social Security and how that should be handled.

Taxes, as we've seen, are always with us, and always creating deeper layers of complexity. And finally, we have the legal issues of an estate passing forward to another party, cleanly and without excess tax or other penalties.

Who knows? For any married couple, leaving this life together, at the same moment of the same day, is entirely possible, though we'd hope the occasion would arise through natural causes. Realistically? The chances are extremely low. I like to say, slim to none, and Slim left town. It's all but a certainty any particular married couple is going to be separated by death at some future time.

If you're planning to hike the Appalachian Trail, it will be a little like climbing Mount Everest—a physical feat. You'll prepare for months, and it will take more months just to make the journey itself. But if you're walking it with a partner, and you know that partner may stop and stay behind at some point along the path, you'll want to include that possibility in your plans. It makes a big difference whether you hike through the wilderness with a companion or all by yourself.

The life journey is much the same. In the larger moments of life, I don't like surprises. The best way to handle them is to have a good map of what lies around the next bend and to be ready for whatever's there.

CHAPTER 4

SOCIAL SECURITY

IT'S BEEN SAID THAT "OLD AGE IS NOT FOR SISSIES." AGING makes a lot of demands on us. It's humbling. And at one time, it reduced too many people to dependence upon charity. Those too old to work, if they lacked financial resources, sank quickly into poverty and relied on their children or the kindness of others. This was never more pronounced or true in this country than during the Great Depression.

As a response, in 1935, President Franklin D. Roosevelt proposed a program requiring people to prepare their own economic security through payroll deductions. It was a kind of enforced savings plan with an eye on the future. The 1935 Social Security Act changed forever the way we think of retirement support.

After nine days of eligibility, there were already one million workers signed on for the program. Four months later, 26 million people held Social Security cards.

On January 31, 1940, the first monthly retirement check was issued to Ida May Fuller, age 65, a legal secretary from Ludlow, Vermont. She received $22.54. She lived to be 100, dying in 1975. Mrs. Fuller had worked for three years under the Social Security program. The accumulated taxes for that time totaled $24.75—and up to her death, she collected a total of $22,888.92 in benefits.

Clearly, Social Security plays a significant role in how we prepare for life after labor. Ida May Fuller was the perfect pioneer of this program, because she lived long enough to demonstrate the power of accumulated investment. She retired at a time when medical advances were already lengthening the average lifespan.

Longer life means greater expense. I've never yet met anyone who wasn't glad to begin receiving that monthly check. It comes in handy.

We explored Social Security just a bit in our "Widow or Widower?" chapter, because it's the foundational block of income in retirement. Ideally, we'll have a number of other income streams, but Social Security is still there for those who haven't made other arrangements. The Social Security Administration's actuaries tell us that, as of 2018, a young worker with average earnings, a spouse, and two children was receiving the equivalent of a life insurance policy with a face value of more than $725,000—simply by paying into the Social Security program, which has been shown to lift millions of elderly Americans out of poverty. A few dollars from each paycheck, an attitude of delayed gratification, and our future is much more secure. Of course, as a "financial guy," I could make the argument that saving that money on your own, investing it, and turning it into your own paycheck may in fact result in more income for you and your family, but the behavioral aspect of Social Security and forced savings is hard to argue with. Would you really have saved all that? Would you have invested wisely? Social Security forces us to plan for the future.

Sure, Social Security is popular. What we do need to talk about, however, is the typical series of mistakes people make when it comes to Social Security. We need to think a little more in-depth about this income stream and how we should be approaching it and planning for it.

NO PLAN IS AN ISLAND

The first and perhaps greatest misperception about Social Security is to think of it as a self-contained island, something apart from other investments and income.

On the surface, it seems simple: Here's a program we began paying into when we first launched our careers. The government has held our money as we grew older. Now it's coming back to us with interest, at a time when we need it most. End of story.

Here's the truth: Social Security is a bit more complex than that. It's not an island but something interconnected with your other assets, your overall financial picture, your cash flow, and your taxes. In other words, it's a mistake to assume all that matters is what's written on the check you receive. Some think, "I'm going to receive X dollars each month from now on. Why wouldn't I want that to happen, beginning as soon as possible?"

Yet there are good reasons to look before you leap into accepting monthly payments. There are many more factors in play than simply the sum you'll receive. It's ultimately about the total assets you have, how they're performing, the effect of taxes, and several other factors. All of this requires careful thought.

As we'll see, simplistic thinking can create inefficiencies in the use of your other assets. You need to consider when it makes sense to file to begin receiving your payments, or you could end up creating unnecessary taxes of the type we've discussed in previous chapters. There could be extra income that seems welcome but isn't truly necessary, and therefore means more liability to the IRS. The markets, and how they're doing at any given time, should also play into your decision. As if that wasn't enough, thought needs to be given to your longevity and how that affects the total summation of moneys received from the Social Security Administration.

The key word is efficiency. You want your money to be working for you with peak effectiveness at any particular moment, to bring in what you need and avoid taxes and penalties you don't need.

So the first big mistake is isolating the Social Security decision, rather than considering it holistically. Your thinking should begin with the assets at your disposal. What does your big picture look like? Do you have a half-million dollars? Five million?

Next, what types of moneys are those? Are they in the pre-tax bucket? Are they after-tax? Are they tax-free? Each situation presents different variables that will create different outcomes.

How about pensions? Some begin at age 60, some at age 62, and so on. The timing of these matters, so get the information together, and create a timeline for how much money you'll have and at what point.

After that, you should ask, how much money will we need each month in this home?

That is, on a monthly basis, considering my mortgage, my groceries, my basic utilities and financial responsibilities, my entertainment and recreation budget—all the regular outflow of money from my lifestyle—how much money do I need to be comfortable, happy, and responsible?

Last, consider your longevity or health. Giving full consideration to the financial side of things without an eye to your overall health would be a mistake. It's important to remember that Social Security payments grow the longer you delay or defer them. But you also must consider how many total checks you will receive.

I know what you're thinking: "Brad, I don't know when I'm going to die!" Neither do I. But, using reasonable assessments, given your current age, health, etc., will help determine the optimal filing strategy for your family.

THE MARKET FACTOR

With these questions answered, you've built an accurate picture of your financial situation for the foreseeable future. It makes sense to take one more factor into consideration: the market at this moment in time.

I hope everyone has learned by now that the stock market isn't quite a constant, smooth, fully predictable ride. These last few years, the stock market has been on a prolonged winning streak. But for how long? Nobody knows. Most of us can remember the global financial crisis of 2007 and 2008.

That crisis was unique, but there are other fluctuations on Wall Street at various junctures. If you're considering taking your Social Security payments, you'll want to ask if that particular moment is the best time for you to file—or whether it would pay to play the waiting game a bit longer.

When you were born enters into this decision, too. If you were born before 1950, your full retirement age is 66. If you were born during the fifties, the age will be 66 and a few months. And for those born after 1960, the age of full retirement is 67. This, of course, is the first time you can begin receiving full benefits.

You can actually take checks at the age of 62, but your payments are reduced by a percentage relating to how early you've filed. Whatever your full retirement age may be, from 62 to that point in time, there's a 7 percent guaranteed growth rate in your payment for every year you defer.

Again, it's an example of delayed gratification. You can have some money now—it's always welcome. But if you wait, you can take your payment at a higher rate. That's even more welcome, but it requires patience and an ability to take the long view.

If you continue to defer, from your full retirement age until you reach seventy, there's actually an 8 percent growth rate in your payment. If you do the math, the amounts become significant. So you can see that the decision to activate Social Security payments is a bit less simple than it first appears. To oversimplify this: would you let your investments grow if you knew you would get 7–8 percent annually without fear of loss? I shrug my shoulders as I write this because it isn't that simple but wonderful food for thought.

Let's say there have been some troubling events on the world scene, and the markets are declining and struggling. You and your advisor might then make the decision to turn on your Social Security sooner than anticipated, rather than later. The reason would be that you'd still need your monthly sum to live; if it didn't come from Social Security, you'd be forced to take significant amounts of your money from your investment accounts while the markets were depressed.

Everyone knows about buying low and selling high—this would be a case of selling low. You'd be cashing in stocks at the worst of times. Better to draw the Social Security check in that event. We call this "Sequence of Returns Risk" in the business—a topic so important, the entire next chapter is dedicated to this concept.

On the other hand, perhaps you've always planned on activating these Social Security checks at full retirement age—66 or 67 or somewhere in between. On the other hand, you're following the stock markets, and your investments are flourishing. That never lasts forever, of course, so it may well be wisest to sell while the prices are high, defer the Social Security payments another year, and take that 8 percent guaranteed growth rate.

You win on both sides.

A QUESTION OF TIMING

We've been discussing factors that we can predict and analyze—your assets, your investments, what your full retirement age might be, your lifestyle needs. They're not all fully "knowable," of course. Investments may earn or lose on the market. Even your lifestyle cost is subject to change, particularly when you consider such factors as medical developments.

The only factor you can nail down with precision is full retirement age, which you can know to the day and the hour. But with the remaining variables, there's good data on which we can make calculated decisions.

The greatest of "unknowables," of course, is longevity. We've discussed what it means to have no idea how long we'll occupy the world of the living. If you could tell me your departure date, we could factor that into our calculations, along with the full retirement date, and reverse engineer an almost-perfect retirement plan. Fortunately, one of the nicest things about the Social Security system is that it's as open-ended as your lifespan. Ida May Fuller proved that. She lived to be 100, her payments continued to come in, and she received a remarkable return for the few dollars she'd had withheld. Fun Fact: for Ida May to replicate that on her own, the $24.75 she had paid into Social Security would have had to achieve a 21.55 percent return on investment annually or total lifetime ROI of approximately 92,380 percent. Take that, Bitcoin!

It's also possible in some instances to get it wrong, yet make it right. Let's say you decide to activate your Social Security payments, and the checks come in for a couple of months. Then, for whatever reason, you realize you've made a mistake. Maybe there's a chance to sell some stocks and do really well, and now you wish you'd deferred your Social Security payments and taken the 7 or 8 percent guarantee. It's not too late.

Not everyone realizes there's a 12-month window to change your mind. In that situation, you'd contact the Social Security Administration online, or through your local office, and you'd tell them you want to reverse that decision. Then you'd need to pay them back. You might have received three or four paychecks by this time; after you returned the total amount, it would be as if you'd never filed, and you'd be plugged back into that pleasing growth.

I recall times when our firm has helped people with that situation. One client, after consulting with us, realized he'd moved too early on his check. We got it reversed because, without those checks, there was less taxable income, and we had more wiggle room with the tax code.

We replaced the Social Security income with after-tax moneys, giving us more room to convert their IRAs to Roth IRAs (in essence, paying off the IRS early, at known, and possibly lower, rates). Our client deferred his Social Security to age 70, and the result was that he got his Social Security tax-free instead of paying taxes on 85 percent of his benefit—not to mention the extra growth of his Social Security based on deferment.

The many wonderful compliance officers I have worked with in my career have instilled a healthy fear in me—a fear that forces me to tell you at this point that not all situations are the same. I think this goes without saying, but hey, McDonald's got sued for having hot coffee.

BUT, for this client, you can imagine the difference in his financial picture. He was a pleased client.

TWO OVERLAYS

By now you will have noticed taxes creeping back into the conversation. Yes, the IRS even has something to say about Social Security. And by that I mean, they want to tax it as well.

Most people fail to consider the tax impact on Social Security, but it makes a great deal of difference. And this angle has its own set of rules. The key here is provisional income, which is a formula. The IRS defines it as the sum of your gross income, capital gains and qualified dividends, and nontaxable interest, plus 50 percent of your annual Social Security benefit. Provisional income levels determine the point at which Social Security income can be taxed. If you stay below that threshold, you can receive your entire benefit tax-free. The client I've just mentioned was a prime example.

There are odd aspects to the provisional income and its effect on Social Security. A couple living in retirement on $10,000 per month might pay full-rate taxes on Social Security—85 percent of their benefit being taxed at the federal tax rates. Someone else might have the same income per month during retirement, $10,000, while paying no taxes at all on the Social Security payment.

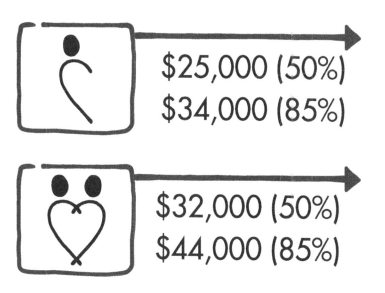

$25,000 (50%)
$34,000 (85%)

$32,000 (50%)
$44,000 (85%)

The point is, it's not about your overall tax liability or how big your paycheck might be. This is very specific to Social Security: it's the *source* of your paycheck, what type of money you're receiving, and where you've saved that will make the difference. The tax overlay must be taken into consideration, and then the stock investment overlay as well.

As I've shown, all these factors affect each other. How are your stocks performing? Would this be a good time to cash them out so that you can leave your Social Security benefits at the more positive growth rate? And what would be the effect on your taxes?

The wrong question is, "How soon can I start receiving that nice check?" We need to ask, "Do I need my Social Security for cash flow? How does this overlay with my personal investments? And what impact will this have on my least favorite uncle—Sam? Simple, right?

THE MARRIAGE EFFECT

A final aspect for consideration is marriage. I could write an entire book on Social Security and all the possible marriage scenarios—past divorce, spousal benefits with an ex-spouse or a deceased spouse, or even a much more common one: married and taking a spousal benefit rather than filing from your own benefit.

In the current generation, husbands and wives are both much more likely than in the past to work outside the home, and either might have the higher past salaries. In yesteryear, of course, fewer women were in the workplace; the man was the "breadwinner" and likely to have the more significant Social Security benefit.

But let's consider that traditional model—a home with a husband who's had a long career, and a wife who took care of the home and the children. The government actually gives credit to stay-at-home parents, allowing the wife (in our example) to take a spousal benefit from her husband's working history. If she lacks a history of earnings, she could receive a benefit equal to half her spouse's Social Security. Again, it's a little-known fact, but a must-know opportunity for those who fit this profile.

The average financial advisor has access to Social Security maximization tools. What do those tools look like? Can we find them at the hardware store? Actually, it's just a fancy way of saying we can take the precise details of your financial picture, place them into an algorithm, and the computer will then spit out 200 or more possible combinations of how to file for Social Security. Then we can quickly identify how you're going to get the maximum benefit at the proper time. Handy tools to have on hand. Any good mechanic or contractor will tell you that you are only as good as your tools.

The numbers don't lie. We simply need to know a client's financial details, figure out the math, then reverse engineer our way into a plan, considering the tax and market overlays. Then that client can rest in the assurance that he or she is getting the best benefit possible for those circumstances. The only variable missing from the equation is the length of life. But we can look at options there, too.

RUNNING THE NUMBERS

Sometimes we run the algorithm a couple of ways. Just for perspective, we run it based on a plain-vanilla strategy (or lack thereof), filing for Social Security at full retirement age, with, let's say, a $3,500 per month benefit. We ignore the overlays and the other complicating factors, and check the financial result for the client after, say, twenty years, when he or she might be in the mid-eighties in age.

Then we run the algorithm again, based on the *best* financial advice and strategies, considering all the variables we've discussed here, the marriage factor, stocks and taxes, and filing for Social Security at precisely the right time.

The difference in these two approaches? Hundreds of thousands of dollars in cash received over a few years. That extra money, under the first option, is just being thrown away. It's as if it's sitting in a bank account with the client's name on it, unclaimed.

Under the second option, however, the rewards are powerful. That money can be left to a beneficiary or beneficiaries in a life-changing way. Or it can be given to a cause that's meaningful to the families we serve.

In the end, this was worked out with an equation—it's math, meaning there's a right answer and a wrong answer. It's not an art but a science; it's not my opinion, but economic truth.

To me, the right answer is always the one that creates the most wealth that can do something good in the world, whether that good is to bring someone comfort and rest, or to achieve something in the world of philanthropy. And how can waste be anything but the wrong answer?

Let's consider a highly affluent person with millions of dollars saved for retirement. Where did that money come from? A lifetime of hard and diligent work. It's the fruit of perhaps 80,000 work hours in 40 years of toil. If this person hadn't cared about the wisdom of saving, that money wouldn't be there. The wealthy person would have found some way to dispose of it.

I don't find that such people are eager to go into retirement without continuing to respect the value of that money. The habits of a lifetime dictate good stewardship, wise financial policies, and leaving behind some kind of legacy that signifies the worth of all those years of labor.

Or consider someone not wealthy at all, someone likely to be a little anxious about the cost of retiring from work life. Things are going to be tight, it would seem. The average check for Americans is a little less than $1,500 per month. For this individual, too, it's hard for me to imagine a lackadaisical approach to signing on to receive that check. She knows she needs to maximize her assets in retirement, and she'll look for every opportunity to gain some kind of financial edge. Perhaps it's as simple as making a sacrifice of some sort to defer payment until that check can be rendered a little larger.

In either case, that person would simply need to understand the facts of the matter. What are my assets? How do our Social Security laws work? How does my marital status affect what's available to me?

What to do with a monthly payment of $3,500—a little more than double the average—is a million-dollar decision. No, I'm not exaggerating. By the time all these factors are slotted into our equations, and the math is run, that monthly payment may represent one million dollars of benefit. I wish more people realized that. I don't know any of them who would tell me, "Brad, put down your calculator. I'm sure your algorithm is interesting, but I figure I'll just take the check."

CHAPTER 5

SEQUENCE OF RETURNS

HENRY AND ART WORKED FOR THE SAME COMPANY FOR YEARS. They were the same age, and they'd been friends for as long as they'd been coworkers.

Both men made stock investments. But since they used different investors, the strategies were different. At lunch time, they were often found in the office breakroom, eating their sack lunches and sharing a copy of *The Wall Street Journal.* They competed in a friendly way over their stock gains and losses, much like other men did with their football teams.

In general, they both did well with their investments. But they noticed something interesting—something kind of reassuring, really. One year Henry's stock would surge, and maybe Art didn't do quite as well. Henry would pull ahead with his investments. But the next year, it might be the opposite, and Art would be on top.

Given enough time, the ups and downs of the stock market tend to even out. Just about the time both men were preparing for retirement, their competition happened to be a tie. They had learned that it didn't matter who did well and when; things even out.

That is, until retirement. Then the two of them unlearned everything they thought they knew.

At retirement, Henry and Art both got their affairs in order. Each figured out he needed about $8,000 per month to live, plus or minus. They made arrangements for their Social Security checks. And they began to cash in stocks as needed, to help account for the cash they needed to live. At that point, their portfolios moved in two different directions.

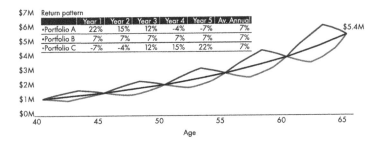

Return pattern	Year 1	Year 2	Year 3	Year 4	Year 5	Av. Annual
•Portfolio A	22%	15%	12%	-4%	-7%	7%
•Portfolio B	7%	7%	7%	7%	7%	7%
•Portfolio C	-7%	-4%	12%	15%	22%	7%

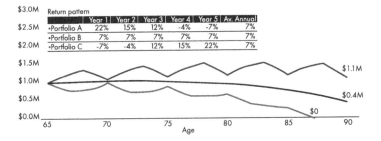

Return pattern	Year 1	Year 2	Year 3	Year 4	Year 5	Av. Annual
•Portfolio A	22%	15%	12%	-4%	-7%	7%
•Portfolio B	7%	7%	7%	7%	7%	7%
•Portfolio C	-7%	-4%	12%	15%	22%	7%

Henry did extremely well *early*. By the time he died, 15 years later, he was worth one million dollars and bequeathed a sizable legacy to his children.

His friend Art attended his old buddy's funeral. Art was broke, in debt, and on Medicaid. And he simply couldn't understand what Henry had done that he hadn't.

The answer is explained by the sequence of returns risk. The two graphics below depict the story of Henry and Art. The first graphic is an example of savings years and the second is an example of spending years or retirement.

Market timing, which was relatively much less important during their work lives, became critical the moment they retired. The stock market has always been cyclical, and the best advice has always been to be patient and hang in there when our investments take a hit. But after retirement, the order of your investment returns, or sequence as we call it in the business, can create huge differences.

In Henry's case, things worked out. Whoever advised him did a good job, or perhaps he was just a little wiser or more patient, or just a little luckier with his stocks. But for Art, certain declines just after retirement, combined with his anxious cash withdrawals, sent his portfolio into a spiral from which he never recovered.

To hear this, of course, is to feel our blood pressure rising. It sounds frightening. But once again, the second scenario—what happened to Art—is not the result of mere chance or the cruelty of fate. It came through poorly timed strategies. We can't control the stock market itself, of course. We know it rises and falls, and what goes up must come down. But we can run various scenarios and preview different likely outcomes, and we can create a strategy far more likely to result in the prosperity and comfort that Henry enjoyed.

FINDING A COMFORT ZONE

Ray Dalio, the billionaire investor and hedge fund manager, suggests the two best strategies appear, at first glance, to be quite simple: number one, stay invested; and number two, avoid large losses.

When you think carefully about these rules, you realize they're really not that simple. If you retired during the last big downturn, you'd be more than a little tempted to react in knee-jerk fashion. Your portfolio would have been severely weakened. You'd want to dump stocks quickly, lest you lose the remaining value. Being patient can be very difficult.

And "avoid large losses"? How exactly do we do that? We do it, of course, with the best understanding of the market and the most rational, unemotional market responses.

But perhaps the real key is the one most often ignored. In my opinion, that key is to be invested in a way that fits your stage of life. If you're 30 years old, healthy, and have your life before you, there are risks you can take and long-term strategies that make sense. You can be more aggressive in your younger years.

If you're at or just before retirement, it makes sense to have a more conservative portfolio—perhaps to avoid putting everything on Bitcoin or a hot tip from a buddy down the street, who's hawking a trendy tech startup.

Still, it comes down to comfort level. All of us are different. Some have nerves of steel and thrive on the challenges of the unknown. Others are bundles of nerves. And most of us, of course, are somewhere in between.

Perhaps you've shopped for one of those beds with adjustable "sleep numbers." They solve a problem married couples have experienced for many years—one likes a good, firm mattress, and the other needs it softer. We're all looking for the fit that's "just right." I call this the Goldilocks Complex. The newer beds are popular because there is no "right number." It all depends on who's doing the sleeping, right? No one wants to spend eight hours feeling "sort of" comfortable; it's important to have it just right.

I suggest taking the same philosophy to your market involvement. Find your comfort zone and invest accordingly. Be certain your investor understands what those comfort levels are and stays well within them. When the market goes up, everyone is happy; the sun shines on us all. Only when it rains do the leaks matter. Several times for every retiree, there will be those moments of challenge, when leaks expose cracks in the roof. Past decisions will be questioned, and there will be uncertainty about how to go forward.

Earlier in the book, we discussed the fact that this is a behavior transition we need to acknowledge. Old habits die hard. Henry and Art were stock market junkies. They watched the markets every day, and for years, looked for great new investment tips. I'm sure it was difficult for them to curb those impulses at age 67 and begin what I call "playing defense." In that earlier chapter, we talked about moving from saving to spending. But we've also moved from offense (an aggressive growth attitude) to defense (protecting what you've built). We'll say more about the defensive mindset below. It will certainly mean being patient with the market and understanding the sequence of withdrawals.

OUT OF THE GATES

In 2002, a racehorse known as War Emblem won the Kentucky Derby and then the Preakness. If you follow that sport, you know there's incredible excitement when a horse wins both races in the springtime. It means that horse has a chance to win the Triple Crown of thoroughbred racing. Only 13 times has that happened, and War Emblem only needed to win the Belmont Stakes to be part of that elite group.

War Emblem's odds in the first race, the Kentucky Derby, had been only 20-1, but he jumped out to a lead right out of the gates and maintained his lead all the way to the wire.

At the Preakness, War Emblem naturally entered as the favorite. But this time he paced himself a bit more, hanging back until the middle of the far turn, then putting on an impressive burst of speed to make up four lengths and win. That's tremendously difficult to pull off among the fastest horses in the world, and War Emblem's legend only grew.

Then came the Belmont—disaster. War Emblem stumbled coming out of the gate, almost to his knees, and quickly fell behind. A fast start is essential in any race. War Emblem exhausted himself trying to make up lost ground, and eventually came in eighth. The next year, the heralded animal was retired to stud.

Why are we talking about horse racing? Because it presents the perfect picture of what can happen with a sequence of returns.

The point at which you retire is significant. Are the markets up or down? The years 2007 to 2009, for example, weren't the best years to retire—yet some were forced to do so, as companies went under or cut their payrolls. Retirees might have found themselves stumbling out of the gate, with assets tremendously diminished.

In a race, the horse with the fastest start has a tremendous advantage for winning. It doesn't always happen that way, though, as War Emblem proved in that second race. It's all about pacing. But a fast start and the inside track certainly offer the best opportunity.

But what if you stumble, even fall? The race isn't over; it's just far more challenging. The point of retirement is the starting gate for the remainder of your life, and we can significantly bolster our chances of doing well by jumping out to a fast start. If the market is strong at the moment (as it is during the time I write these words), your portfolio is strong and growing. As we all know, the markets can hit the proverbial iceberg at any time and suddenly find themselves sinking. If you've just recently retired, that's problematic, though not hopeless.

The difference between retirement and the years preceding it is what Henry and Art experienced as they compared stocks during their working years. The market went up, it went down, and in time, it always corrected itself; as financial analysts say, it reverted to the mean. Stumbles were just part of the rhythm of the market.

Retirement is different; average rate of return is no longer the focus. There's far less time remaining for things to average out. The race is not a marathon now; like the thoroughbred races, it's full sprint, and stumbles are disastrous. The other significant factor is you're now making withdrawals, pulling money out at a time when your shares have lower value—which means, of course, you have to pull out more of it. And to pull out more is to borrow from what was meant for tomorrow.

TIME AND THE MARKET

The market is something you can't control. What can you control? Theoretically, how much money you have and how much you're saving each month. At least you bring those variables to the table on your own. As for the market, what you're hoping for is a good, average rate of return. You're going to begin spending your money now, and the market value of what you withdraw doesn't have to be at its peak, but it should at least be at an average return. These distributions begin to affect long-term outcomes.

Imagine you're 65 years old, you go ahead and retire, and you begin to set up monthly distributions from your investment account to live on. During the first two years of your retirement, the markets sink. Perhaps they were surging when you retired, you felt good about things, you planned accordingly, and now the markets are correcting themselves. Your portfolio is weaker than expectations.

In these two years, you've taken 24 paychecks through a monthly recurring draw to supplement your Social Security and reach that figure you've decided you need every 30 days. You notice that with each withdrawal, it's a loss. That means that, for all intents and purposes, you were locking in those losses and accepting them. That dollar, pre-retirement, always had the chance to grow back and replenish its value. Withdrawals take away that chance. The money is going to be spent at its real-time value, which is less.

Time is always the key to the market. When I speak of investing, I actually assume having five-plus years to allow dollars to take advantage of long-term market growth. There has to be time to allow for peaks and valleys to even out. If we're talking about less than five years, I don't call you an investor; I call you a gambler. That's the importance of timing, and Ray Dalio understands that when he says to stay invested. Time is your friend and helper unless you lose faith and panic.

But the other advice Dalio gives us is to avoid large losses. How are we supposed to do that? The answer, as we've said, is to play defense.

PLAYING DEFENSE

As we've established, you think like an offensive coordinator in the first part of life. The object is to rack up points, right? You want to be aggressive, to attack, and to continue running up the score. You might lob a few passes sixty yards downfield to the endzone. You take some risks.

But in retirement, you have to train yourself to think like a defensive coordinator. If you know football, you realize that's a complete opposite posture. You're moving from attacking to protecting, from an unstoppable force to an immovable object, hopefully. It's the fourth quarter now, and you've built a nice enough lead to win the game. If you continue to run a lot of high-risk offensive plays, these could backfire, and you could let the enemy (financial calamity) back into the game. Now you're on defense, and it's about protecting your lead and no more.

So in market terms, how should you get into a defensive posture? Here's the difference between football and investments: there is no clock ticking down on the scoreboard. We don't know whether we're going to be on defense for 10, 20, or 30 years.

You're protecting your investments for an open-ended period of time, so you must be that much more conservative. For example, you can't have your money sitting in cash the entire time (hiding it in the mattress or keeping it in a coffee can buried in the backyard). That's not really protecting it at all—it's devaluing it because of inflation. Your money shrinks in time. So the barest of necessities is to keep up with inflation.

If, then, you need your money to grow, even if it's just to keep up with inflation, that means your job isn't *purely* defensive. You still must protect the full value of what you have. After 30 years of retirement, the amount you need each month is likely to be a different number, because the cost of living has increased. But how do you do that in a way that is still defensive-minded—so that you're first and foremost protecting your money, but also keeping an eye on its growth?

The simple answer is that you stay invested. Can you do that during a time such as what we saw from 2007 to 2009, when the market S&P dropped 53 percent in a 16-month timeframe? Can you do that at a time like the onset of the COVID-19 panic, in March 2020, when the world was shutting down indefinitely?

These were times to batten down the hatches, so to speak, stay in the market for the duration of the storm, and avoid risks that might be uncomfortable. If you go to cash, you're taking cash not only from the present but from the future, since it will never have the chance to grow back to its former value.

WHY WE GET IT WRONG

When I was working to gain my securities license for the first time, I took what's known as the Series 7 General Securities Representative Qualification exam. All advisors must pass this test if they aspire to do fee-based and commission-based consulting. For a youth pastor, as I was at the time, this was an intimidating program of study, a lot to know, and I had basically no background for it. Not only was I a youth pastor, but I had grown up with a single parent, and virtually no money. I was a raw rookie who hadn't exactly spent my life preparing to enter this field.

So for me, it was an anxious moment. A number of years have passed, and I don't remember every item on that test. But one subject is lodged in my memory forever: the odd lot theory. It tells us to watch what the average lay investor does, do the exact opposite, and we will make money. According to theory, the small individual investor is usually wrong.

I thought, "How can that be? Is it because people are stupid?"

No, not at all. Small investors are probably, on the average, at least as intelligent as everyone else. The real reason they're so often wrong is they invest based on feelings rather than intellect.

Feelings are good things to have. Individual emotions are what make us human and give us a distinct personality. But combining emotion and investing is like putting two kids in the nursery with one shiny toy. They're just not going to get along. There's going to be a lot of crying.

Maybe in TV or the movies, you see stock investors who make millions on some kind of market ESP, a natural feel for things, which leads us to believe that since we have gut instincts, too, maybe we could be fantastically successful investors. But this script doesn't play out much in the real world. When the stock market tanks, the average investor feels a lot of emotions; something in him cries out, "Sell! Sell before your shares lose all value."

Watch what that investor does, and do the exact opposite—which is usually doubling down on patience.

After all, if you make the decision to pull out, your judgment has to be right not once but twice. You must be right on when to get out, and then you must be right again on when to get in. That's a much dodgier strategy than riding out the storm. As a matter of fact, what tends to happen is that people get out, based on their feelings, and then find they're forever too antsy to get back in. For every national market crisis we've had, we've seen people panic, go to cash, then find themselves still there many months later, after a market correction, when it's too expensive to get back in at the same level.

Our advice is always to stay invested. But to do that, of course, it helps to know your limits. Think again of the bed with the comfort control. Know your number: at what point do you begin to feel uncomfortable? When you set up a financial plan for retirement, your advisor needs to know that limit and work within it. If the advisor talks you into a plan that's likely to keep you on edge, you won't stick with it.

So the advice here is the same advice a good dietician might offer you: go with a plan you know you can enjoy and maintain comfortably. For daily meals, an all-green diet may make lots of sense. But if you happen to hate most of the vegetables on it, you'll abandon that diet fairly quickly. You need a financial plan that keeps you invested, that plays defense, but that also works well within your comfort zone.

Maybe that's what happened with Henry and Art. Henry did very well, had no problems with sequence of returns, and his portfolio prospered. Art, on the other hand, got hammered early, panicked, and went to cash in a way that damaged his future prospects. Perhaps the plan placed him beyond his level of comfort. Then, when he finally cashed out completely, he never had the courage to get back into the market and ended up with nothing. Those of us who are advisors are committed to prevent that scenario.

One of the reasons for Art's anxiety would have been longevity. How many years would he need to keep drawing a check? What if something happened to him next week? What if he lived to be 100?

That's our next topic of discussion. How do we plan for a mystery—perhaps the greatest mystery of all, how much longer do we have to play in this wonderful game we call life?

CHAPTER 6

LONGEVITY

WHAT DO YOU THINK OF WHEN YOU HEAR THE WORD *OLD*?

It's funny how our perspective on that issue changes in the course of a lifetime. When you're a child, teenagers seem *really old*. Not much different from adults, really.

Even as a young adult, you look at those in their forties and think, "Look at those wrinkles!" For you, that's so far off in the future, it doesn't even seem real.

History affects these things, too. If you'd lived during the time of Julius Caesar, your life expectancy, *if* you survived birth (many didn't) might be your late thirties. Even 100 years ago, the average life expectancy was only the late forties.

I remember watching NBC-TV's *Today* show in my early years. Willard Scott had a segment in which he would recognize people "90 years young," or maybe, on a really special day, a sweet elderly lady having her 100th birthday. Traditionally, centenarians have received a special letter from the president.

Yet today, one study shows that the number of people reaching the century mark (known as centenarians) is growing by a staggering 5 percent every year. That status is no longer particularly rare.

We've already talked about Ida May Fuller, the nation's first Social Security beneficiary, who lived to be 100 years old. Yet when President Franklin D. Roosevelt's administration established Social Security, the program was designed as an end-of-life benefit. The retirement age was 65, and perhaps people would draw those checks for a handful of declining years. No one foresaw a three-decade payout.

Yet here we are, with Social Security front and center as a foundation of retirement finance, and the program itself is endangered by the number of people living long enough to receive decades of checks.

We know that with advances in medicine, most people have longer life expectancies. We're seeing real progress in fighting cancer, and we have a better understanding of what constitutes healthy life, exercise, eating, and so on. In the UK, it was announced a few years ago that one of every three babies born in 2013 is expected to reach 100 years of age.

You and I might both live to enjoy a triple-digit birthday. It's much less unlikely than you think.

Even so, longevity is no less a personal mystery than ever, and always will be. We simply don't know the span of our own lives. And it's something that affects every other topic we discuss in this book—just like taxes. Maybe that's why we have that expression about death and taxes being inevitable. We never escape either, even in financial planning.

Longevity is a critical element of our calculations. How can we best approach an unknown variable in terms of financial security during retirement? After all, the longer you live, the more likely you are to develop new needs, including health-related concerns; the more money you need; and the more inflation complicates your financial projections. The list of complications goes on and on.

CHANCES ARE

There's an aspect to life expectancy that I believe most people miss. Think of the flip of the coin. There's a fifty-fifty chance it lands on either side. If you plan on a life expectancy of about 85, as some clients do, you're looking at a 50 percent chance of your death being on one side of that age or the other. If you come out on the plus side—well, you've run out of plan.

We don't approach many things with an eagerness to choose something that could be decided by the toss of a coin. Planning for retirement does involve considering risks. We assemble a plan that's cognizant of the various risks in your life. As a matter of fact, most of the chapters in this book are based on risks: the sequence of returns risk; the tax risk; the widow/widower risk; and so on.

Risk and chance—we think of the scene in *Dumb and Dumber* in which Jim Carrey asks a beautiful girl (Lauren Holly) about the chances someone like her could end up with someone like him. She tells him the chances aren't good. He insists on odds, and she says, "One in a million."

An excited Jim Carrey says, "So you're telling me there's a chance! *Yeah!*"

We laugh because if Jim Carrey weren't "dumb," he would quickly walk away from those odds.

But we're not talking so much about astronomical odds as we are close ones—fifty-fifty-type chances. Most of us have traveled by airline. We find our seats on an airplane and pay mild attention to a flight attendant who explains what to do in case of a crash. We know quite well that if this plane goes down over the sea, all the floatation devices and emergency exits in the world are unlikely to help us. There aren't many activities that place us closer to death's neighborhood than soaring above the clouds at jet speed.

But most of us are relaxed, calm, and ready for the flight because we know the chances of dying in an airplane crash are one in the tens of millions, depending on whose projections you use. Statistically, it's one of the safest places any of us could be. Driving in traffic is a higher risk, as we've all been told.

But imagine walking up to the jet bridge, preparing to board. The pilot is standing there, and you stop to chat with him. You say, "How's the flight shaping up?"

The pilot thinks for a moment, then replies, "One of the engines is kind of 'iffy' lately. I'd say we have about a 90 percent chance of landing."

Ninety percent? That's a lot better than 50-50. But would you board the plane? Not me—I'm out of there. I'm on my way to look into Amtrak or perhaps a more reputable airline. There's a low risk and a high reward to flying—you can travel great distances in a short time. There's an acceptable risk and a high reward to driving—you can move all about town and beyond.

Yet many people envision retirement plans that extend to the age of 85 or something similar. It's how we see ourselves. Many clients offer stories of how their parents and grandparents died at a certain age, and they expect they'll last about that same length of time. But what if they live to 95, with 10 years uncovered? Or even more?

I also think there's something about the male ego in play. Perhaps men don't like to think of themselves living these long lives, less active, enfeebled by old age. Perhaps it's the well-known fact that women have slightly longer life expectancies.

None of that means a man won't reach 90 or older, though. As I've said, living past such an age as 85 is more like a 50-50 proposition. Are you willing to make a plan that only extends to a certain age, when it's just as likely you'll outlive that plan?

What's at stake? Your plan could end, and your Social Security checks and pension checks will continue. But so will the taxes on each. So will your medical bills, perhaps with long-term care expenses. All the things you pay for on the other side of 85 will still be there, but you'd now stand a strong chance of running out of money. So do you want to fly with that particular plan, if you have such a large chance of the engine stalling before you land? Will you brave the longevity risk?

LIFE POINTS

Actuaries use what they call a "life table." It shows, for each age of someone's life, the chances that person will die before their next birthday. Sure, it's a bit morbid, but somebody has to keep track of these things, right?

There's a lot of data out there, and the data allows us to find out a certain number of facts about a person—their age, their gender, their health, their occupation, and so on—and project their resulting life expectancy. In the life insurance world, as you probably know, this kind of information helps the company to assess risk.

It's far from a likely scenario that one or both of you dies at the age of 85, or any particular age, for that matter. It's an unknown quantity, the drawing of a number from a hat. The question is whether any of us wants to gamble on that—to say, "Well, I think we'll be gone by this or that particular age, and I'll bet all my assets, all my wealth, on that."

Looking at the cold, hard reality of the data, we can conclude that if you want to have a very strong chance of success that your plan is a good fit, that you planned long enough and didn't outlive your plan—you would have to plan to the age of 100 and maybe a little past it. We know from statistics that a certain percentage of people will indeed reach the century mark.

Or looking at it another way, if you plan to retire in your early-to-mid-sixties, you have 35 to 40 years of planning that needs to be done. I've never had the desire to jump out of a plane with a parachute that stops working before I touch the ground!

One reason some of these age numbers may be surprising, I should note, is that we're accustomed to seeing averages for the general population. But financial planners don't calculate based on the world average, any more than you buy clothing designed for the average human dimensions. No one ever comes into our offices and asks for a boilerplate financial plan; they want one geared precisely to who they are.

If they're people who have accumulated wealth, people with a decent education and from a certain background, that places them in a certain demographic in which the numbers are a bit different from those of the general population. Members of this demographic have access to better healthcare, for example. Life expectancy is extended in those circumstances.

In designing someone's custom plan, we would also want to take into consideration family history. We do want to know about your parents, their health history, and how long they lived. But your personal situation is far more important. What kind of environment do you live in? What kind of healthcare do you access? What's your job and its stress level? What's your state of health and its history?

If you happen to be the kind of person who has positive answers to most of those questions, and indeed the type of person likely to have saved for retirement and to be ready to create a financial plan for retirement—you're in that group that's likely to enjoy an extended life expectancy. The last thing we'd want to do is create a plan to 80 or 85 and leave you exposed after that.

It seems crystal clear that we need to rethink our idea of long life, at least if we're making serious plans.

I've mentioned that I see my mission as showing people how to have a good time—to stop saving and start spending. That's an enjoyable mission to have. I'm helping people be less anxious and more eager to embrace the remainder of life with the money available to them. But I can't imagine calling a client to wish him a happy birthday as he turns 85, and talking with him about the end of his financial plan. "I'm sorry you outlived your money today," I'd say as he blew out all those candles. "We knew there was a pretty strong chance of this."

You might sadly tell me, "We were too conservative with my plan."

And I'd reply, "Actually, we weren't conservative enough." Because in financial planning for retirement, the literal meaning of "conservative" is *assuming a long life*. Being conservative involves being cautious and risk-averse. It's not cautious to gamble on running out of money. To be conservative is to stretch your money to a safe distance, based on the reality of your probable lifespan.

OFFLOADING THE RISK

Sometimes these risks for retirement can be offloaded in advance. For example, the longevity risk can be diminished through insurance policies. It's what we do when we worry about an automobile accident and buy auto insurance. We don't worry about a bad storm coming through and ripping the roof off our house, because we've bought home insurance. The house is covered by the roof; we're covered by the policy.

Social Security is already doing that for us. All through our working years, we've offloaded the longevity risk by paying into a plan that would generate monthly income for the balance of our lives, regardless of how long those lives may extend. Theoretically at least, Social Security is an income stream we can't outlive. (We have some work to do to make sure that program is around for the next generation, but it's solid for those now retiring.)

Pension payments work the same way. If you served in the military and qualified for a military pension, it will always be there for you—*always*. For example, this may be hard to believe, but Irene Triplett was living in a North Carolina nursing home just before her death in 2020, and collecting the last Civil War pension—$877.56 annually from the Department of Veterans Affairs. She was born in 1930, the daughter of an 84-year-old soldier who fought for both sides during the war. Even she couldn't outlive her pension.

Offloading risks gives us peace of mind. With insurance policies, there are some who pay more in premiums than they'll ever get out; others receive a $30,000 check on a wrecked car after making one small payment.

Other than for one chipped window, I've never filed an insurance claim on my car, but I've paid faithfully for years; I'm on the losing end of that game. But that's alright with me. I don't have to drive around with the thought in the back of my mind that there could be a calamity, and I'd lose my car and all its financial value.

We have Social Security and other pensions to help us offload some of the risks, but we can elect to go a bit further. Your insurance company will build a deal with you that allows you to make payments. Live as long as you'd like. If you outlive your money, they have to keep sending you a paycheck as long as you're breathing. It's a bit like Social Security or a pension, but designed more personally for your needs.

This is simply an annuity—a series of payments made at regular intervals. Some people have overcomplicated the definition of that word, but it's rather simple. In this case, it's nothing more than income insurance. All kinds of extras can be added—investment angles and so on—but those are just the details. The true value of an annuity contract is the assurance that as long as you live, there will be money coming in the door.

For those who look at all these risks—sequence of returns, tax, market fluctuations, medical care, and the rest—longevity insurance is the best way to ensure peace of mind. You're going to spend your money, you're going to enjoy your life, and you're not going to wake up in the middle of the night terrified that your Social Security check has been nullified by inflation, or the market has plunged, or you'll need some medical procedure that is too expensive. At the front end of retirement, you took a hard look into the future, you made arrangements, you've paid in faithfully, and you've bought some genuine peace of mind.

NEITHER GOOD NOR BAD

There really are only two reasons to buy insurance. One is for a risk you don't want, and the other is for a risk you can't afford.

We work with some people who have a certain amount of wealth. They drive nice cars, and if those cars were totaled tomorrow, they could simply walk into a showroom and buy a replacement with cash. Yet they write checks for automobile insurance every month, and not just because the law requires it. Their thinking is, "Why should I have to pay tens of thousands for a new car, when I can pay you $50 per month, and you'll then have to pay *me* the tens of thousands?" It's not that they can't afford the risk; they'd just rather not worry about it.

There are many among us, however, who can't afford the risk. We're willing to pay for medical insurance because we know there could be a catastrophic event in which we couldn't afford to pay for our care otherwise. We could need prohibitively expensive cancer treatments, or open-heart surgery. Group policies are highly expensive today, but we're willing to pay them because we can't afford even the slight possibility of what the risks entail.

We talk to people who have already heard a lot of advice. They've heard that this or that kind of annuity or payment is good, or it's bad. None of these options are qualitatively good or bad—they're simply options, ways to get paid that may or may not work for our needs and preferences.

The Social Security and pension checks will keep coming. They're not subject to market conditions, and that could give them more value or less. But it's still neither "good" nor "bad" because it's all wrapped up in what we personally need and expect and what keeps us in good spirits through our retirement years. Like the mattresses we discussed in Chapter 5, there is no correct comfort level. The answer is different for each person.

The issue at hand is, do you need income? And how much? Do you value the guaranteed payments because you can't afford not to have them, or because, on a behavioral level, you'd rather move on with your life and not have to think about them?

Please realize that many of these decisions are less about the details of the options than about the details of your life and mindset. That's why firms such as ours spend some time getting to know you, rather than pushing boilerplate policies your way. We understand your goal is to comfortably finance the remaining years of your life, but it's also for you to have a comfortable mind—even if you live to be 100.

Speaking of which, how do you figure out the right withdrawal rate when it's possible to live that long? That's the subject of our next chapter.

CHAPTER 7

WITHDRAWAL RATE

IN THE OLD COMIC BOOKS, SCROOGE MCDUCK—DONALD'S uncle—was the elite billionaire of his time. He owned a massive vault where all his money was stored. Apparently, he didn't believe in investment—just an immense stack of currency, gold, jewels, and every kind of treasure. He loved nothing better than diving into the pile like a pool, rolling around, and luxuriating in his wealth.

I don't recommend that you keep all your wealth in one vault, for obvious reasons. Shame on Uncle Scrooge for not getting better financial advice. But just for the sake of illustration, imagine you have a locked room with all your assets inside. There's a pile of all your money, perhaps a bit smaller than Scrooge's. A machine cranks out your monthly Social Security check.

There are also lockers for your various pensions and annuities. An old-fashioned stock ticker, the kind in a little glass dome with ticker-tape scrolling through, shows how your investments perform. It's rigged to deliver cash just like the automated teller at your bank.

This room is the financial fortress of your future, your money pantry for the retirement years that stretch forward in time. But once it's built and ready to operate, you have to make a decision. You can pay one visit to this room per month to retrieve what you need.

"Well," you think, "that's no problem. I'll just grab a little extra each month, in case I spend too much."

But upon further review, you realize that's no good. If you keep taking a little extra, month after month—well, deep down, you know you'll spend it, right? Just having it tempts you to use it. You could run out way too soon. You feel a tinge of panic as you picture the room swept clean, and cobwebs where all the riches used to be.

And that raises the question, how much do you actually *need*? Maybe you could just find out how much *most* people like you need, and go with that. But again, you realize that's no good. Even "people like you" all have different particulars. If you were Uncle Scrooge, the answer would be, "Take as much as you want!" (Though Scrooge himself was a miser.)

On the other hand, if you didn't save particularly well, and had nothing but your Social Security to rely on, you'd need to ration money like water in the desert.

The answer is relative to who you are and how much you have. But you keep glancing over at the stock ticker and realizing it's relative to other things, too, right? If you have investments, and you're staying in the market, you really have no way of knowing what the future holds. You'll presumably have some dividends, but they could make you a prince or leave you a pauper.

And then, as if things weren't complicated enough, there's that question of how long? How many months will you be making this monthly trip to the vault? That question is huge.

How long are you going to live? Everything depends upon that! You could be here for four more years, or even forty. That won't affect your fixed monthly annuities, such as Social Security and pension—though the longer you live, the more cost-of-living increases could come into play.

The first question, of course, is what do you *need*? Based on the lifestyle you expect, and the expenses you anticipate, how much money is the base requirement?

Hopefully you've saved enough, and planned enough, to cover that figure. But you don't want to be overly cautious, and miss out on trips to special places or other perks; neither, perhaps, do you want to spend every penny. You might want to leave a legacy to your children (if we're honest, it's really all about the grandchildren these days) or to charity.

EVERYTHING UP FRONT

You've probably daydreamed about how you'll spend your retirement days when you no longer have to go to the office or storefront. You imagine days on the golf courses, leisurely lunches with friends, maybe a month-long trip driving across the country or a cruise to Fiji. Planning those activities is one thing. Making financial plans for retirement is a whole different animal. You must understand the exact challenges you face. At what other time are you asked to create a 30-year plan and totally commit to it, so that you'll either perish or prosper based on how that plan works out?

Never. It's something new to all of us.

I like to describe the challenge by describing this little scenario. It's utterly unlikely, sure—yet it captures what we're facing.

Imagine you're 22 years old and you've been hired for your first job. It's a good position, with moderate pay, and you're excited to report for work on that first day. You meet your supervisor, go over your responsibilities, and finally you ask, "How often will I receive my paycheck? Weekly or every two weeks?"

Your employer laughs and says, "This company isn't like all the others. We're giving you all your money right now—your total salary for the next 30 years. You'll be signing a contract to work with us for that full period, of course. You'll be locked into that contract. But you'll be treated very well and paid well. It's just that we're going to hand you all your pay, 30 years' worth of salary, right up front. Here you go: $1.5 million dollars."

Your head would swim, wouldn't it? A check for $1.5 million?

Like any of us in that situation, you'd be thinking about everything that money could do, and could do *immediately*! You could go ahead and pay cash for the finest car, and get rid of the aging lemon you're driving. You could buy a fantastic home, wear some sharp suits—you'd be living the life, wouldn't you?

But then you have second thoughts. It's three decades of salary, and there will be no more; that money had better last. Thirty years seems like a long way off, but what happens if you have a really good time, then run out, say, 10 years early? Because with the purchases and activities you're imagining right now, that's more than possible.

The company wouldn't care. They'd say, "We gave you your money. What you do with it is your business."

So your realization is that you'd better make it last. You have to come up with a plan to live within your means and stretch that money to be absolutely certain you don't run out. Because "running out" means out on the street, and still owing that company years of work!

Is this story really so far-fetched? It's a word picture of retirement planning. When we see a sum of money, we think about what we can do with it right now. It's only human nature. We're accustomed, from long years of life and work, to assume there will always be more money. We spend it, we make some more.

But once you retire, that's no longer true. What you've got is handed to you. It's up to *you* to decide how and when you spend it—but there won't be more, for the most part. And there may be 30 years or even more to spread out your spending.

The immediate problem is, how much money can you have right now—a month from now? The month after that?—without endangering your future?

That's the question that firms such as ours work through with our clients. Everyone will have different answers, but even so, there's an industry-standard answer for the question of "how much can I take?"

And that answer is 4 percent. Why? And is it a good answer? We'll get to that presently. But first, let's look at some basic math.

CRUNCHING THE NUMBERS

I've described the algorithms we use to figure things out, and some of them can be pretty complex. There's a lot of math involved, and I did promise this book wouldn't be boring! I know a few people who don't enjoy math, particularly since it's so cold and hard. Mathematics is what it is; it tells you what it tells you, and it makes no exceptions. Frankly, this is precisely why I like math. My pragmatic brain revels in the certainty and linear nature of it.

But some of the math is actually very simple. The most basic formula that's given to the public for computing a safe withdrawal rate is as follows. It actually works from the starting point of how much you know you need per month.

Safe withdrawal rate (SWR) =
annual withdrawal amount ÷ total amount saved

You might have $1 million saved—a nice, round figure. You've checked all your expenditures, mortgage debt, "fun" money, and just a little for a rainy day, and you decide that what you need is $2,500 per month to live comfortably. That works out to $30,000 annually.

Here's how the simple equation would work out:

$$\$30,000 \div \$1,000,000 = 0.030, \text{ which is } 3.0 \text{ percent.}$$

That would be a simple starting point. The math says the number you'll be drawing from your pile of cash is 3 percent, which most advisors feel is on the safe side. (The industry standard is 4 percent.)

Of course, you'll notice it doesn't take longevity into account. It doesn't take sources of income or other factors into account. But it's a handy tool, and it can help your thinking. Some people look at the equation and think, "I could change that by finding a way to cut my expenses right now."

Or perhaps they think, "I would really like to take a little more money each month, so that means I need to increase my total assets. Let's sell the house, move into something smaller, and invest the difference."

But again, the rule of thumb that planners tend to go by is known as the 4 percent rule, a kind of universal one-size-fits-all withdrawal rate. Where does it come from exactly?

"SAFEMAX"

William P. Bengen is a retired financial advisor, and he's the man who popularized the 4 percent rule of retirement savings. I'm not sure whether he considered it simpler than rocket science; the fact is, he *is* a rocket scientist with a BS in aeronautics and astronautics from MIT, so he's a smart man. He's successful in several fields but is best known for creating Bengen Financial Services and popularizing the rule we're discussing. His article on the subject is entitled, "Determining Withdrawal Rates Using Historical Data," and it appeared in the *Journal of Financial Planning*. I readily admit this is bordering on boring, but hang with me here, I'm just setting up my right hook.

The idea caught on quickly, mostly because it was simple, because it seemed sensible, and particularly because he did some impressive homework. If a retiree draws down no more than 4 percent of his assets on an annual basis, he concluded, that person should be in no danger of outliving his money.

In time, he gave his theory a name: the Safemax rate (safe maximum). But over time, he began to hedge a bit on his conclusion. He suggested the number might actually be a more robust 4.5 percent for tax-free money, and 4.1 percent for taxable. And as long as inflation stayed low, he felt, the number might even be higher.

Using the simpler 4 percent figure, we'd give this example. If you had $1 million in your IRA, you could spend $40,000 the first year and tweak the annual withdrawal upward just enough to match inflation. And you'd know you were on safe ground.

Of course, there were reams of historical data on stocks and bonds to support this contention. Bengen used a 30-year time frame and ran 10,000 different simulations of different market scenarios, assuming a 60/40 blend portfolio (60 percent stock/40 percent bonds). He produced his 4 percent conclusion with a 90 percent confidence rate.

By the time he diversified his conclusions a bit, others were already voicing their reservations with Safemax. Time had passed, and some skeptics pointed out that Bengen had done all his research during a time of much higher interest rates on stocks and bonds. That created rosier projections than some felt were warranted.

Wade Pfau, PhD, is a Professor of Retirement Income at the American College of Financial Services. He wrote that Bengen's research, placed in the context of today's financial realities, would point to the safe withdrawal rate being 2.4 percent rather than 4 percent. That's a significant difference. It would mean that, with the $1,000,000 IRA, you would take $24,000 the first year rather than $40,000—$2,000 monthly rather than $3,333. That could mean the difference of a monthly mortgage payment for your dream home or an annual trip around the globe.

The debate rages on, but in my industry, the most common rule of thumb is still the 4 percent figure. Most of the time, in fairly ordinary circumstances, it seems to work. We can leave the experts to quarrel about the precise percentage rates, but either way, we're left with questions we can't answer: how long will we live? The percentages are based on averages in various scenarios.

Keep in mind, Bengen was giving us 90 percent confidence in his conclusions. If we go with his figures, we're going to accept a 1-in-10 chance of being wrong. And here we go again with our airplane scenario, from a previous chapter. Are you willing to climb onto a plane that has a 90 percent confidence rate for landing? Not me, and probably not you.

It's highly improbable that anyone will come up with a 99.999 percent confidence rate on an answer for your retirement plan—air travel–type confidence. There are just too many variables involved, and we live in highly exceptional times anyway. In this century, we've seen news events we never could have imagined, each one leaving its mark on Wall Street. We couldn't have expected the crisis of 2008; neither could we have expected the prolonged surge of recent times. The only thing we can be certain about is uncertainty.

I wouldn't base my plan on a nearly-30-year-old study and the conditions of those times anyway. Nor would I base my plan on a boilerplate percentage guess with a boilerplate plan. I wouldn't bet my life on a convincing article online, or listen to a buddy down the street. I want to think more carefully about the full picture, the best advice I can find, and then base my plan on my situation, my comfort level, a good valuation of my assets, and a conservative approach to what the future may hold.

INFINITE SCENARIOS

As we've stressed, everyone is different. We have clients with our firm who go with 6 and 7 percent distribution rates. You might have paid attention to all we've said and conclude theirs is a dangerous approach—these people are going to run out of money!

Yet these are cases in which clients don't have 30-year timeframes. They're more advanced in age, so it makes good sense to pull more than the common 4 percent. We have to consider whether someone is living without some of the enjoyment they could be having due to a 4 percent rule of thumb that may not apply in their case. But if you've been highly successful—enough that you're able to retire at the age of 55; even if your health is strong; even if your stocks are performing well and your family has a history of longevity— regardless of all that, you want to be on the conservative side. You have a lot of years ahead of you.

What about someone who retired in 2009, just as a 12-year period of surging stocks began, and the market was up 400 percent? Sequence of returns is on her side. She'll probably be fine. Yet if the same woman retired two years earlier, in 2007, she would probably soon be broke because her first distributions took severe losses. It was all locked in, and that's a hard road of recovery.

Those are simply aspects of timing. We know that's one aspect, but our personal situations, how much money we have, and what the sources of it are also enter into what the withdrawal rate should be.

Sometimes clients have already heard about the 4 percent rule, and their friend thinks it's a great idea, so they come in set on 4 percent monthly distributions. But if it were that simple, of course, you wouldn't need professional advice. Instead, we recognize that every situation is different, and every situation is impacted differently by an uncertain future.

PERCENT CHANCE YOUR ASSETS WILL LAST THROUGH YOUR RETIREMENT

INFLATION-ADJUSTED WITHDRAWAL RATE (%)

	20-Year Period Stock/Bond Allocations (%)					30-Year Period Stock/Bond Allocations (%)				
	20/80	40/60	60/40	80/20	100/0	20/80	40/60	60/40	80/20	100/0
1	90-100	90-100	90-100	90-100	90-100	90-100	90-100	90-100	90-100	90-100
2	90-100	90-100	90-100	90-100	90-100	90-100	90-100	90-100	90-100	90-100
3	90-100	90-100	90-100	90-100	90-100	90-100	90-100	80-90	80-90	80-90
4	90-100	90-100	90-100	90-100	80-90	40-50	50-60	60-70	60-70	60-70
5	70-80	70-80	70-80	70-80	70-80	0-10	20-30	30-40	40-50	50-60
6	20-30	40-50	50-60	50-60	60-70	0-10	0-10	10-20	30-40	30-40
7	0-10	20-30	30-40	40-50	40-50	0-10	0-10	0-10	10-20	20-30
8	0-10	0-10	10-20	20-30	30-40	0-10	0-10	0-10	0-10	10-20
9	0-10	0-10	0-10	10-20	20-30	0-10	0-10	0-10	0-10	0-10
10	0-10	0-10	0-10	0-10	10-20	0-10	0-10	0-10	0-10	0-10

0% to 10%
Confidence is very low; significant changes to goals may be necessary now and into the future.

10% to 70%
Confidence is moderate to low; you may want to adjust your plan.

70% to 90%
Confidence is sufficiently high without undue sacrifice; changes to goals are likely to be minor and manageable.

90% to 100%
Confidence is high; may imply unnecessary sacrifice to lifestyle or undue investment risk. You may want to adjust your plan.

BlackRock, Inc. is the name of the largest asset manager in the world. Recently this company produced a safe withdrawal rate chart that has become very popular in the industry, because it took an approach different from some of its predecessors. Instead of a massive study with a 30-year time frame and a 90 percent confidence rate—as helpful as that was—the BlackRock approach used a sliding scale that followed the money over time with various draws: 4, 5, 6, 7, and 8 percent. Each draw was charted in a different color, so it was possible to get a dramatic picture of exactly what would happen to the same person using various withdrawal rates.

The earlier version of the chart showed the example of a 65-year-old retiring in 1972, and followed his money through the years up to 2002. Again, the various colors of lines looked somewhat like airplanes climbing into the sky. But only the 4 percent line stayed aloft in that chart. The retiree taking 4 percent started with a million and ended up with $2.5 million at age 95—a nice legacy. The 5 percent "plane" crashed in the retiree's late nineties—he was broke. The higher draws all crashed earlier. It was clear the retiree who drew 4 percent was leaving enough in the market not only to go the distance but to make him a lot more money.

A later version of the chart is plotted differently. The retiree begins in December 1999 with $500,000. Then we have those colored lines representing various sizes of withdrawal. At the end of 2020, after some time recovering from the 2008 market crisis, with 4 percent draws, the retiree still has a little bit more money than he began with. At 5 percent, he still has $300,000. With higher cash draws, the retiree crashes at earlier stages.

Other charts help us see the results with various portfolio mixes—how much stock, how much bond, etc. These are the details that can be studied to ascertain exactly what kind of scenario you bring to retirement, and what you can reasonably expect with your own investments. The next few years, of course, won't be exactly like the last few years. There was a crash in 2008, a slow recovery, and then a powerful surge. Those things aren't predictable, but using computers, we can run huge numbers of scenarios and discover the range of possibilities.

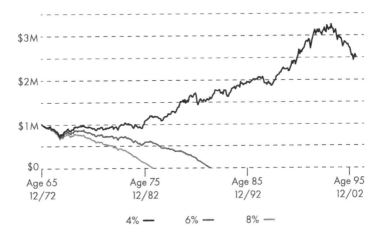

$3M

$2M

$1M

$0

| Age 65 | Age 75 | Age 85 | Age 95 |
| 12/72 | 12/82 | 12/92 | 12/02 |

4% —   6% —   8% —

What should be apparent above all is just how crucial that monthly withdrawal rate is. The difference in taking out 4 percent and taking out 5 percent may not seem like much if you haven't done your homework. If you have $1 million, and you draw 4 percent per year, that comes down to $3,333 per month. If you decide to draw 5 percent, it's $4,167 per month. You look at the difference, and it doesn't seem like much: $834. When you know you have a million, you might think, "Surely I can use another $800 without feeling guilty about it."

But the difference over time could be stark. In one scenario, you end up with enough to pass on to your heirs; in the other, you go broke and end up living on assistance. It's important to do everything possible to find that "Goldilocks" number—not too hard, not too soft, but just right—especially knowing there are looming challenges that can't be predicted.

Among the most unpredictable is the challenge of healthcare.

CHAPTER 8

HEALTHCARE

CERTAIN CONVERSATIONS ARE OFTEN LOADED WITH FEAR AND uncertainty. When we talk about our future in combination with the topic of healthcare, we access those feelings. We all have our stories—some our own, some from our families. Someone we know had a healthcare event that was a struggle physically and even financially. Since it touches everyone on a personal level, it carries that emotional weight.

We can talk about taxes rather unemotionally, even though we hate taxes. We can discuss Social Security and the rate of withdrawal, no problem. Even the prospect of becoming a widow or widower is a subject we can probably handle, though it's discouraging terrain.

But the idea of healthcare costs in retirement terrifies a great many people. Even if they've accumulated a certain amount of wealth, they can imagine the rising costs of hospitals and doctors eating up all that they've carefully, sacrificially saved for so many years. We've seen all those hospital bills, and we've had no clue how they rose to those staggering prices. That Ibuprofen cost *what*?

It's really expensive—that's all we know. And then there are the frightening prospects of long-term care and the loss of basic abilities they've taken for granted all throughout life. Getting older is one thing; becoming frail and immobile is another.

It's common to say, "Well, it won't happen to me." Yet the US Department of Health and Human Services tells us that today's 65-year-old has nearly a 70 percent chance of needing long-term care services sometime in the future. And a private room in a nursing facility costs $8,821 per month, according to the Genworth Cost of Care survey. The weatherman may tell us there's a 70 percent chance of rain, and we joke about how often they're wrong; yet we take an umbrella after hearing that percentage.

This isn't the weather we're discussing. This is life. It doesn't take much imagination to envision what could happen in the case of checking into long-term care. A lifetime of savings would be signed away, month by month, to some bland, cheerless facility that represents the one destination we most yearn to avoid.

No wonder we don't want to talk about it!

But please don't stop reading. I get it; there's a human impulse that makes us want to blurt out, "Can we change the subject?"

By the time you finish the next few pages, I believe you'll agree there's very good reason to have these conversations, and very strong strategies for facing the challenges we talk about.

Past the age of 65 or so, even if we've taken exceptional care of our bodies, we begin to feel our age a bit. We may need knee-replacement surgery or lower back treatments. We may have to turn to daily pharmaceutical medications we'd never have imagined a few years ago. We find ourselves getting to know various doctors and specialists quite well.

Aging makes philosophers of most of us. We think back on childhood and the boundless energy with which we attacked life. And we realize that, in some ways, life moves in a circle. We began life as infants, limited and helpless, with our entry to this world being quite a financial expense to our parents. As we grew, we became more independent, capable of walking or running, speaking intelligently, and thinking quickly. Somewhere in young adulthood, we peaked. We came of age, and were filled with vitality and ideas and enthusiasm.

Then, quite gradually, we began to move in the other direction. We'd climbed Mount Everest and realized we were on our way back down the slope. We lost a step or two. For the first time, our kid beat us in one-on-one basketball. The first gray hairs arrived, the first wrinkles not too far behind. And eventually, as the years mounted, we found ourselves in need of assistance again, just as when we were very small. We struggled a bit to speak, like we did in early childhood. A lifetime ago, our parents helped us to stand on our own two feet. Now, it's our own, grown children who are bracing us as we take our hesitant steps.

It's the circle of life. We understand. What we'd like to avoid, though, is what often happened a century ago: seniors were forced to move in with their children. Their financial resources had vanished. They worried constantly about "being a burden," and particularly with the constant doctors' bills and the special care they required.

Taxes and healthcare costs are the two greatest financial challenges to a peaceful retirement. The first, at least, is somewhat predictable. It follows a set of laws, and we can build our strategies around our understanding of the tax system and its requirements. Healthcare, on the other hand, is an open-ended challenge. The healthcare system itself is constantly in flux, and of course our healthcare needs are unpredictable, too.

We enter retirement with big plans. Life isn't over—just the main work phase. My entire business is built on the premise that you should thoroughly enjoy this period of your life, and that we're here to help you do that. It's party time; we mean that. But even as you begin to plan that month-long trip to the British Isles, or shop for an RV, or perhaps buy a second home, you know there's this whole other financial area we'd rather not spend time thinking about: the cost of taking care of our physical health. Quite often, some of us require a great deal of coaxing to begin a serious discussion of this part of our future.

There's no need to dwell on the negative aspects of aging. We do need to remember that all the various topics in this book are given attention in order to set up boundaries within which we can have freedom. For example, we've discussed withdrawal rate. The boundary there is how much we can safely draw from our collected wealth each month, enjoying ourselves within those limits so that we can be financially free for the duration of life, and also be free of anxiety that the money is going to run out. We'd be remiss if we didn't discuss healthcare, given the place it plays in life now and for the rest of life.

We need a plan that prepares us to handle all these challenges. The two dominant issues, however, are clear: Medicare and long-term care. But for some, there's an earlier question: What if you retire early? How will your healthcare needs be met then?

RETIRING BEFORE 65

First, the age of retirement certainly matters. If you're fortunate enough to retire before the age of 65, there's a transition between the company's healthcare plan you've enjoyed and Medicare, the national health insurance program. It normally begins at that age. For some with certain medical conditions, it could begin a bit earlier.

Retiring before 65, there would be a gap to fill in between the employer-sponsored plan and Medicare. You might need to go find your own plan for the interim. So your first task would be finding out what that costs, and where the best plan would be available.

As always, how it ties back into your taxes is a factor, too. It's your taxable income that determines whether your healthcare premiums are going to be subsidized. In other words, there's a tax break; there are people between the ages of 55 and 65 who have retired and have healthcare premiums that are fully subsidized. It's all based on their modified adjusted gross income.

So taxes and healthcare become intertwined at this point. To be purposefully redundant, I'll remind you this book isn't designed to get into every nitty-gritty detail of the tax code. Just know that if you retire before you're 65, you need to talk to somebody who understands the tax angle. Premium tax credits are a strong strategy. These ultimately came about as a result of the Affordable Healthcare Act. You can write off taxes based on your income estimate and certain household information you provide.

As of this writing, you can't be denied healthcare in our country, but that can always change. What it means is that no matter what pre-existing conditions you have, no matter what the state of your health might be at this point in time, you're going to be able to get healthcare insurance. The question is whether it fits into your budget.

At 65, you do get Medicare, but that's not as simple as people often think; it's not like flipping a switch. There are multiple pieces to it, so that coming into retirement, you need to understand what is covered and what the premiums really are.

MEDICARE

This chapter won't tell you every single thing you need to know on this subject. As a matter of fact, I'm not a Medicare specialist. But I can point you down the right road, so that you can find someone who is a specialist and can help you piece the whole puzzle together.

Medicare is divided into four parts: A, B, C, and D. C is actually an alternative, Managed Medicare, also known as Medicare Advantage. The primary parts are A, B, and D.

Medicare Part A is what everyone receives automatically at the age of 65. Most of us happily exclaim, at this point, "It's free!" The truth is, we've been paying for it for many years. Your premiums have all been processed, and you get the benefits. Part A covers hospital, skilled nursing, and hospice services.

Medicare Parts B and D have not been included in our payments, so those have to be bought with premiums based on our income. B has to do with outpatient services and professionally administered prescription drugs. D covers self-administered prescription drugs.

On Parts B and D, if your income rises above a certain level, Income-Related Monthly Adjustment Amount (IRMAA) charges are added. The Social Security Administration places us within four income brackets. The numbers may have changed since this book was published, so you're better off Googling the current rates. The rule to remember is that if your income rises above certain levels, your premiums will rise as well.

Here again, taxes matter. Modified Adjusted Gross Income (MAGI) will determine what you pay in premiums for Part B and Part D. At the risk of contradicting myself and getting a bit too far into the weeds, it's worth noting that your MAGI that determines your Medicare premiums in your current year comes from your tax return two years previously. As an example, your 2022 Medicare Part B premiums will be determined from your MAGI of 2020. I know, nothing can be simple.

Keep in mind that Medicare is like a leaky roof. It gives you some coverage; it keeps out the hard rains. But there are holes where some of the wet stuff gets in, and you need to plug those holes. How do you fill the gaps where Medicare fails to cover certain needs that may arise?

Independent brokerage can be helpful. That's not one of the services in our firm; we're not involved in healthcare plans. But a good broker might be able to help if you're intent on filling the gaps between the Medicare Advantage plans (Part C) and the Medicare Supplement Insurance, or Medigap.

The Medicare choices you make aren't exactly a slam dunk. That is, you shouldn't sign up for Medicare Advantage just because a friend of yours did it and recommends it. As with everything else, your personal details matter. Get good advice from someone who can study your specific situation and show you the advantages and disadvantages of these options. There are complexities—let's just say that if we're climbing or descending the mountain, this is one of the most treacherous passes. You don't want to take it on without a good mountain guide who knows the territory.

I once heard comedian Jerry Seinfeld, in one of his stand-up routines, say that all men see themselves as "low-level superheroes in their own world." And the example he gave was out on the highway, where you'll see a guy driving along with a mattress tied to the roof of his car. He's apparently bought this great, thick mattress, and invariably he has his arm out the window, holding down the mattress. The guy believes, "If this rope snaps and the wind catches this huge rectangle at 70 mph—I got it! I got it! Don't worry about it. I'm using my arm!"

That's the way some of us can be with these heavy questions. We're moving along through life with the issues hanging over our head, and we think we've got it covered. We figure we have superpowers that will kick in if need be. But if that heavy wind gust comes through, it's not just a problem for us; it's a problem for everyone else on the highway. Our actions affect others.

Healthcare in retirement is a heavy, looming issue. If there are sudden needs, you're going to want to know everything's really tied down well; everything's been covered by good planning.

Even writing this book in the proper sequence was difficult because where do you begin? We started with tax. You can't do tax planning without an eye on Social Security and Medicare. But you can't handle Medicare without taking into consideration how your income distributions are going to be set up to create your paycheck. It doesn't matter if you're going to retire before the age of 65, or if you're retiring after 65 and looking to fill in the gaps of Medicare with some sort of supplement; it's worth your time, energy, and effort to get the most comprehensive picture of all your options and possible strategies.

For example, if you go to a health insurance broker, a policy purchased through that broker costs the same as if you found and bought it on your own—but you've gotten professional advice. You actually have the ability to get professional help at no cost. I don't know why anyone *wouldn't* take advantage of that fact.

LONG-TERM CARE

Particularly as we live longer, and as medical advances increase our longevity, we find the need for long-term healthcare. It comes in many forms, responding to the almost infinite needs that may come up. But the greatest obstacles are, first, our reluctance to think about it in advance, and second, our resulting lack of preparation to handle the financial side of it.

As I've met with people over the years, I've observed how uncomfortable people are with this one aspect of retirement planning. Yet there are a few who are not only willing but anxious to talk about this subject: those who have seen and dealt with this issue in the lives of their parents or another family member. They've seen what can happen to someone who hasn't made the proper preparations for late-life healthcare needs. The questions that arise can tear families apart as disagreements arise. I've seen people lose the family farm because the finances simply weren't there.

Anyone who has been through something like that understands the need to make a plan, and to make a plan early. As a matter of fact, that's often the spark that encourages them to set up a visit with us. I've often heard statements like, "I can't stand the thought of my children arguing over this, or taking money out of my grandchildren's college funds so that I can hang around a few more months with the nurses and the bedpan."

Others haven't seen such things. The issues seem more distant, and it's easier to avoid the subject and think, "That's not going to happen to me." And if that's the case, they're likely to have some misconceptions. When they hear the words "long-term care," they think immediately of the phrase "nursing home."

There may not be a more unwelcome phrase in the English language. Something close to 100 percent of the population will say, "I don't want to go there. I won't do that." As we all know, the time may well come when they have little choice in the matter.

I've had multiple family members who entered long-term care. My grandma was one of those great ladies with a powerful will—I'll just say it, she was stubborn. But the time came when she couldn't take care of herself any longer, and she had no choice but to go into a care facility, no matter how much she protested. As a young child, I'd go with my family to visit her, sit at those round card tables beside the couches covered with plastic, the ever-present birdcage in the corner, and we'd play cards with my grandma—King's Corners. She would do two things constantly: cheat and complain about everything related to that nursing home: the other residents, the staff, the food, you name it. It wasn't a positive experience for her, and I doubt it is for most people. But no matter how much she was against it, no matter how strong her will, that was the hand she was dealt. To my grandmother's credit, she never lost her will to complain. She did that until her final days.

When we discuss "nursing homes," we're often thinking in terms that have long since become out-of-date. They've changed quite a bit since I was visiting my grandma. Once the options were to stay in your own home, move in with your children, or go to the long-term care facility ("nursing home"). Now there are countless options, in stages: your full independence; check-ins at your home by qualified care specialists; full-time helpers at your residence; having your home retrofitted for your specific needs—and then the options of various kinds of facilities. A great deal of attention is given to maintaining someone's dignity and providing attention to what they need and want.

There are also insurance policies available that aren't limited to the traditional long-term care facilities. They agree to cover pretty much any kind of qualified care you might need. They might pick up something as simple as retrofitting your bathtub, your stairway, or other parts of the home that become more difficult to navigate. They might cover part-time or even full-time care specialists who are geared to your needs. By planning in advance, you set in motion the plans that make all of this possible.

As for today's care facilities, they're not based on "confinement," which is the word that summarizes our fear about these places—our basic human claustrophobia about being limited to a small room and perhaps an apathetic nurse who checks in every now and then and treats us indifferently. They're driven by what they call the activities of daily living (ADLs): six basic activities—bathing, dressing, eating, transferring (bed to wheelchair and back), continence, and use of the toilet.

If you can't perform two of the six, insurance policies will kick in and help with your expenses. "Being put away in a home," as some phrased it, is a much more distant option than it once was.

HAVING THE CONVERSATIONS

In the care industry, there's a great emphasis on allowing us to age gracefully and with dignity. In the end, that's what most of us want. Beyond that, we should mention a third concern is a no-frills, pain-free death. Most of us envision ourselves perhaps passing away quietly in our sleep, sometime before we get to a stage when life's freedoms—to move, to think clearly, and so on—slip away from us. We may not get that wish. There may be decisions a family must make together in terms of end-of-life choices, and it's important to have those discussions sooner rather than later, when matters can be considered unemotionally, and of course, when the individual himself or herself can be part of the decision process.

Assets need to be part of the discussion, too. If we think about seeking help from the state, we need to keep in mind that, before you can qualify for this aid, you'll have to have spent all your personal assets. You'll be left with next to nothing before the state steps up to handle expenses.

As for escaping that by giving things away in advance, most of those loopholes have been closed. You could pass your rare coin collection to one of your kids, but you'll find there's a five-year look-back over your assets. If they find you've given away something of value in that period, it will have to be paid back. Most people find this a shocking intrusion into our private affairs, but it's simply the state of things.

The key word, then, is *timely*. Tomorrow always seems like a better date to have difficult discussions. Tomorrow never arrives—but the day does come when it's too late. I'm sure that, as you've read this chapter, you've realized just how many subjects there are to address with your family. One good, comprehensive plan can ward off tremendous heartache, family divisions, and of course, the loss of your resources. It's quite a feeling of freedom to realize the hard questions have been handled.

I also imagine you've discovered once again just how intertwined all the elements of retirement are. Your Medicare premiums, which will be the greatest portion of your health coverage in retirement, will be tied to your income, which is based on your taxes, which are tied to how your assets are set up, which is tied to how you've saved those assets, which is tied to your basic lifestyle. It's a lot of ties to unravel, and sometimes it's difficult to know quite where to begin. I would say, begin with a good family conversation. Talk about values. Talk about the future, your dreams as well as the things you'd dearly like to avoid. If you work with a financial advisor, these should be discussions you are having with them. And if these subjects *don't* come up, you need to ask why. They're too urgent to avoid.

As you have these conversations, and as your deepest desires for the future come into focus, you'll also think of one final piece to the puzzle—the one that we don't qualify as a "risk" but, instead, a wonderful opportunity, the one that comes directly from the heart.

Our final topic in this book is the subject of giving.

CHAPTER 9

GIVING

I'VE ALREADY TOLD YOU I LIKE MOUNTAINS AND THOSE WHO climb them. I like rivers, too. There's just something majestic and transcendent about a river.

A couple of years ago, my family and I were visiting the northern part of Minnesota on a church trip. Someone told us that Lake Itasca, the headwaters of the Mississippi, wasn't too far away.

The starting point of one of the world's great rivers? There was no way we weren't going to check that out.

"Headwaters" is just a fancy way of saying "the source." So this would be the very source of the Mighty Mississippi, the river above all others that most defines the United States. Its massive watershed drains all or parts of 32 US states and two Canadian provinces. It's basically the spine of America—the way we know east from west.

I was excited to see where the Mississippi sets out on its journey and ready to have my breath taken away. I wanted to feel what I might at the Grand Canyon or watching a sunrise over the ocean.

We were, well, underwhelmed—at least, based on our expectations. We found ourselves staring at a marshy little pool, surrounded by trees. This was how the Mighty Mississippi set forth? With all the riverboats, the massive arching bridges, and all? *That* Mississippi?

We live in the Twin Cities, so we know this river. It flows right through the east side. We know it's wide, deep, and powerful as it rushes by.

That really got me thinking about how a force of nature more than two thousand miles long, that chops right through a great continent, can start out so small, so unassuming. I guess it's actually one of mother nature's favorite tricks; you and I started out kind of tiny ourselves!

But movement makes the river what it is, right? Its power is contained in its forward momentum. You always find the rapids where the water is moving the quickest, and that's also where the water is cleanest and clearest.

But there are other parts of the river that detour into little inlets, where all the moss and dust and bacteria congregate, along with every kind of mosquito. It doesn't even smell very good. Maybe you've gone fishing or boating and found these unappealing little coves. The waters that go there lose their momentum and grow stagnant.

Maybe you've figured out where I'm going with this. I've found that wealth flows a bit like a river. It starts small, but becomes a powerful force, pushing forward, cutting its course through the world to affect a great many people. But once it stops moving, once our money just sits in an account or a pocket—that money becomes stagnant and lifeless.

Or maybe we're the ones who grow stagnant. Money is meant for more than sitting in accounts and reproducing itself. It's restless. It wants to get out and do things. In other words, it's a reflection of who we are.

THE EXTENSION OF LIFE

This is one of the great reasons we give: generosity brings life and meaning to what we possess. We see our wealth working in the world, doing something other than simply making more money. In so many ways, we can use that money to make the world a little better place than the one we initially found. We can bring pleasure to people we know or even people we don't. Given wealth and the needs around us, the opportunities are nearly infinite.

There's also the idea of legacy. The river of life always pushes onward. It flows into the future, into a world we won't live to see. Sometimes we wonder, "How will I be remembered? Will I be remembered at all?"

We hope for eternal life; some of us have faith our souls will live on. But we can make certain that our work in the world continues on for generations, in tangible ways. Giving is how we ensure that. We can create trusts and foundations that will regenerate through compounded interest and impact the world far beyond our personal horizon.

Some of the great millionaires of a century ago are still amazingly active in today's world—the Rockefellers, the Carnegies, the Lillys—still forces in society, because they made plans to give not only into retirement but beyond the grave.

But philanthropy, which means "love of humanity," isn't solely the domain of millionaires. One of the great stories of personal benefactors is that of Oseola McCarty, who, in 1995, established a trust to provide scholarships for deserving students in need of financial assistance at the University of Southern Mississippi. She left $150,000 to seed that fund. Her source of wealth: washing floors all her life.

Oseola lived her life in what we'd consider something close to poverty, as a domestic helper in Mississippi. Even so, she'd been trained by her mother to be frugal. She never owned a car, for example, and simply walked where she wanted to go. But all this while, she continued placing most of her weekly pay in a simple bank account. The bank took notice after a few years, as her wealth grew, and officials offered to help her plan her estate and take care of her money.

They also talked her into enjoying life a little bit. Oseola finally allowed herself to purchase some window air-conditioning units and install cable television for the first time.

An attorney for whom she'd done laundry stepped up to help Oseola plan the dispersal of her estate: 10 percent to her church, a little for a few relatives, and the bulk of it to the university. When the news broke, local leaders quickly funded an endowment to honor her. This is another way we multiply the benevolence of our use of money: we inspire others.

Finally, Oseola McCarty set up a trust and received a monthly check until her death in 1999, remaining happy with a relatively simple life and the knowledge she was doing something good for the world—something bigger than herself.

OUT OF THE BOX

I like to look at things plainly and simply, and my view is this: You can only do two things with your money once you're in that retirement phase and in the crowning years of your life. You can't take it with you—we all know that—so you really have two remaining options.

One, you can spend it on yourself. You can have as much fun as possible. Simply disperse your wealth for pleasure and enjoyment.

Two, you can give it away—to family members, to others, or to causes you're passionate about.

We're conditioned by our times to think the first option is the most desirable, the most enjoyable. We made the money, and we should have all the enjoyment of it. You've seen the bumper sticker: "He who dies with the most toys wins."

Yet I could give you a long list of people I've known who will make the opposite case. The greatest joy of their lives hasn't been spending on themselves, collecting toys, traveling, or throwing parties. No, what really continues to give them exuberance and vitality is seeing how much good their money can do for others. There's often some pet project, some worthy cause that has captured their hearts, and it's become a new reason to get up each morning. They travel. They plan. They see the fruits of their giving, and there's nothing they could buy that would match that feeling.

Their money is flowing gracefully into the future, rather than becoming stagnant.

I've heard a comparison of life to a game of Monopoly. You play the game, you collect a lot of paper money, maybe some real estate, and at the end of the game, even if you win—it all goes back in the box. The implication of the story is that it's all "play money" in the great scheme of things, and it's only for this life.

I have a slightly different take on that. I may go in the box, but my money can still do some things after I'm gone. The older I get, the more I see the value of giving and helping my clients do the same. The financial planning world, my field of operation, has become deeply focused on helping people grow their money. It's an art and a science, and many of my colleagues do it very well.

But I believe many of us have lost sight of teaching people how to spend it rather than simply protect it and grow it. Greg Boyd, the pastor and theologian, has said, "The curious thing about money is that it only acquires real lasting value when you give it away." Monopoly doesn't teach you to do that, by the way. You buy, you sell, but in the end you just put it all back on the shelf. Giving it away and bringing joy to others is much more fun than any board game.

FILLING OUR CUP

Many financial planners simply don't think in these terms; we're not trained to do that. I came into this industry *green*—a shade of green reserved for the nicest fairway at the nicest golf course around. I went to school for ministry—youth ministry specifically. Not exactly a ton of financial advising courses were needed, if you know what I mean.

So, I needed all the training. Everything the industry had, I needed. The firm I started with trained right out of the Certified Financial Professional (CFP) manual. The amount I learned on giving and generosity was almost zero. It's not that my colleagues are against generosity; I'm sure they'd all agree that giving is one of the world's greatest experiences. They've just focused so consistently on the saving side of things, they've neglected this other side.

I've seen it over and over: the happiest people on the planet are the ones who have found significant ways to use their means to impact the lives of other people in a positive way.

Some of them say they're more excited about what they're doing now, through philanthropy or mission, than what they did for forty years of career work—even though they were incredibly high achievers and attained fame and prominence. Seeing clean water wells drilled in Africa, or scholarships established at their university, or research funded to combat Alzheimer's Disease, gives them a thrill that beats all their old business victories. Simple donations made to their local place of worship or their high school have serious and meaningful impacts.

I think it also touches us in some deeper part of the soul. We may all share different spiritual beliefs, but I imagine we can agree that none of us can fill our own cup. We spend most of our lives pursuing fulfillment, searching for some meaningful connection. We have a drive to find contentment. That's not a religious doctrine, just observable human nature.

But in the end, all our attempts to fill the cup are unsuccessful. Nothing we do strictly for ourselves or our family seems to bring the fulfillment we seek. What we *can* do is help fill the cups of others—it's rather ironic, isn't it? Only when we give do we truly feel we've received. I believe we're just wired that way as human beings.

Another theme of this book has been the fact that we have no true freedom without boundaries. In my line of work, we help to create those boundaries that provide freedom. We draw lines where there have been no lines, and people can be far less anxious. They know, for example, that if they draw so much money per month and no more, they're not likely to outlive their money. They know how things will work once their spouse leaves this world, or once they pass away and leave a spouse alone, and they feel settled.

Giving is one more example of this freedom. When people know their boundaries, when they understand how much they have and how far it will go, they're free to give more than they ever dreamed or anticipated. The other side of that coin would be living with the fear of going broke—then there would be no freedom for generosity or for anything else. They'd miss out on this joy because the boundaries were too obscure. Retirees would have to clutch their possessions all the tighter, not knowing how long they'd have them.

It's a wonderful feeling of freedom when we can stop clinging and begin sharing. We learn that we can enjoy not only the personal use of our money—for travel, for personal projects—but we can see the joy others experience as we share with them.

I believe in the intrinsic good of all people. I believe that in our heart of hearts, we all want to be generous, and to give and bless others with the resources we have. I also believe the thing most likely to keep us from doing that is *fear*. "I don't know how much of my own resources I will need," we think, "so I don't know if I can give."

It truly makes me sad to think that the only thing that could stand between you and a work of generosity that could not only bring joy to others but fulfillment to you is fear. Maybe this is getting a bit personal for a book of this type, but this one really hits a personal chord.

THE POWER OF NOW

As we meet with the families we serve, one of the most common dreams that is shared with us is, "I would like to leave a legacy."

That comes after we've assured people we can help them manage their resources in such a way that they never run out of money while they're alive. That's the first order of business—will we have enough?

Once they know they're provided for, clients are free to think about the idea of legacy. They might say, "I want to leave something for my kids." They envision the reading of a will or trust, sometime after they've passed away.

But I always respond with this question: "Wouldn't it be a lot more fun if you gave it away while you were alive? Wouldn't you enjoy being around to see it?" We could wait twenty years, to the moment when you're no longer here—or we could start today. Maybe they want to bequeath X amount of dollars to a charitable cause. I ask, "Is there any reason you shouldn't do that now?"

I ask my question, and sometimes people have that bewildered look on their face—*can we do that?*

"Why not?" I ask.

"Well, I guess—because I don't know whether I have enough to do that now."

Yet by now, I bet you can answer that objection. It all goes back to the planning process, doesn't it? If you look back to the previous chapters in this book, you'll see that each risk we've discussed can be met with a solid plan. And yes, all these risks are interrelated; everything is tied in with everything else. Have I said that before?

But think about this. When you have a solid plan, everything also impacts everything else in a *positive* way. If you pay fewer taxes, it helps the other areas. If you get the sequence of returns correct, you've brightened your whole picture. And of course, giving is always helpful to your tax position. So even though that's not the *reason* you give, necessarily, it's another positive that comes out of generosity.

And best of all, a solid financial plan in retirement is like a windshield into your future. You knock away some of the mist and rain, and you see clearly what's ahead. That clear vision allows you not only to give in the future, way down to the bend of the road—but to begin giving now.

And to begin giving now affords you so much more personal pleasure.

Through your plan, you can allow for charitable giving built into your monthly checks and bonuses. You budget these donations as planned expenses, just like your mortgage, utilities, or any other costs of living.

Some have asked about the 2017 tax law reducing our practice of itemizing deductions. But at the magical age of 72, you can make QCDs (qualified charitable distributions) from your IRA. This way, it won't affect your taxable income but will count toward your required minimum distribution.

There are lots of things we can do to help you give, and lots of ways giving will help your total financial picture. QCDs are just one example.

FROM THE HEART

You may have read about Dolly Parton's involvement with various charities. She's been exercising her generosity aggressively, rather than waiting until someday after she's gone. It's hard to know where to begin to describe her varieties of giving.

For years, she's worked to boost literacy and to promote education in Tennessee, the home state she loves. She's participated in initiatives such as the Make-a-Wish Program. She worked with the US Fish and Wildlife Service to establish a bald eagle sanctuary. Then, in 2017, she gave a million dollars to a children's hospital.

When COVID began to ravage the world in 2020, she donated another million dollars to help fund research for a cure at the Vanderbilt University Medical Center—which then became a national and world leader in research for COVID medications.

One of her favorite achievements has been the Imagination Library, which provides one free book to children per month, from birth to school age. By 2018, she had donated 100 million books all over the world. It meant so much to her because she grew up in the mountains, and so few people in her family ever had the privilege of an education.

The total list of her gifts and charities would be far too long for this chapter's purposes. My point is that I'm sure Dolly Parton has thoroughly enjoyed being a celebrity, recording country and popular music, and starring on television and in movies. But I get the idea her true, abiding passion is found in what all that money has bought her in giving power. It's not just more blessed to give than to receive; it's ultimately much more rewarding.

As with all aspects of this book, there are many strategies for giving in retirement. Some of them have been affected by the 2017 tax act, for example. Sometimes, as mentioned, it makes much more sense to itemize than not to itemize. It's possible to donate not just money but stocks or bonds. Many people feel this is the best way to give a gift that keeps giving.

Lots of other options are available, many of them helping you maximize your gift while minimizing your taxable income. But of course, what matters most is not whatever tax strategy you may adopt or however many dollars you may save for your estate; it's the unique feeling of giving something to make for a better world.

I mentioned earlier that I believe there's good in all people, but that fear is an obstacle. Having a plan, gaining control, and setting boundaries will help eliminate that fear and bring about the freedom you need to either increase your giving or perhaps receive the gift of fearless giving.

One of my greatest friends in this life, the one who has challenged me most on a personal level as it relates to giving and generosity, said to me once, "Give until it hurts." My personal journey in life to generosity isn't perfect or straight. But my buddy was right; once you feel a little pain because you were so generous, you will find that "thing," that fulfillment we all seek.

This also happens to be the most rewarding part of my job. I get a front-row ticket to the show. I get to see, up close and personal, the fulfillment and joy that come when people give.

CONCLUSION

NEXT STEPS

STILL HERE? AFTER ALL THESE CHAPTERS?

Good for you. Here's something I often say to people who come to our offices for a visit. "Regardless of what you decide after today—whether you choose to partner with us or not—the fact that you're even here, having this kind of conversation, says good things about you. It tells me you're eight steps ahead of most people, because you're thinking past the moment.

"You're interested in making plans, rather than just living your life for today and ignoring what's around the corner. I can say with strong confidence that things are going to work out quite well for you, simply because you're getting good, useful information and acting accordingly."

Now, that's what I tell people who are willing to *talk*. What about those willing to *read a book* on this subject? That says even more—in *my* book, so to speak.

So you're off to the best possible start as you walk up to the edge of retirement. Now it comes down to doing something with what you've begun to learn. I say "begun to learn," of course, because we've skimmed the surface of a complex topic. Believe me, there's more. There's always more, really.

Your next step is to hire a mountain guide.

We've moved through this book with the recurring word picture of climbing up and down mountains. We discussed the fact that the descent requires a whole different set of muscles and skills. But no matter how you prepare yourself, it also requires a skillful mountain guide who knows the terrain.

Think again about that trip to Nepal, to climb Mount Everest. The ascent and the descent are only part of it. You dreamed about it so long, but when you actually decide to do it, you realize the extent to which logistics are involved. You have to plan. You have to know what kinds of exercises get your body into the proper shape for something so demanding, and how long you need to do those exercises, and so on. You'll need to buy certain supplies, which will be very important. Where do you get climbing supplies? Do you buy them here or onsite?

Then you need to make travel plans, book flights, find a place to stay, etc. You need to know something about medical capabilities in the area, to be on the safe side.

You don't know what you don't know. That's a scary place to be.

With all these things, you need guidance. If you had to do it all completely by yourself, with no help from anyone, the whole dream might drift away from you. Just too much stuff. But you can offload these things. There are people willing to help with each of the tasks we've named. Otherwise, you'd never get it done.

There are travel agents, personal coaches, and people to get you ready and get you there. Then there's that guide who actually walks with you, plans with you, and climbs with you. There's an actual certification for mountain guides that requires a number of proficiencies and a certain amount of experience. You don't want to go up there with someone who's never done this before. At least I know I wouldn't. But the right skilled, vigilant professional can not only keep you safe but help you have the experience of a lifetime.

Financial planners are good mountain guides. If you Google "financial planners near me," you're likely to find a small army of such people. And I would guess most of them would advise you on retirement issues along with all the other areas of money management. But it's like bringing a general mountain guide versus one who only climbs Everest, year after year. Specialists are nice. So it can be an advantage to work with a retirement planning specialist. Even more specific, one that teaches people how to spend their money.

TEAMWORK

There are two common mistakes I see people make all the time. The first doesn't require much discussion: the tendency to do nothing at all.

Some people simply fail to prepare. You'd be surprised how many people actually fall into this category, taking a lifetime of wealth and gambling it on lack of preparation. But as I've said, it's unlikely you fall into that category. If you've signed up for a visit or read a book like this one, you're pretty clearly not someone who leaves it all to chance.

The other mistake is a little more complicated. It takes us back, once again, to the mountain-climbing analogy. What if all those people helping you did a terrible job of working together? Perhaps the personal coach gave you exercises that didn't match what the guide wanted you to do, or the travel agent booked you on a poorly timed flight. You'd quickly see the problem. You would need to make sure you communicated exactly what you wanted.

You'd also need to require your various helpers to communicate with each other and stay on the same page. It wouldn't do to have a lot of independent agents; what you'd need is a team. And perhaps better yet, you would find someone who managed the whole complex project of making an Everest climb and descent—someone who specializes in coordinating these trips.

One issue we run into involves working with clients who already work with a number of professionals. They have a good CPA with whom they've worked for years. They have a money manager or a stockbroker. They have someone who handles health insurance. They have various independent agents. But we find on occasion that none of these agents are on the same page. They're not bad at what they do; they just don't happen to work together.

One of the bedrock propositions of this book has been that everything is interrelated. Tax touches everything. Social Security, timing of withdrawals, stock issues—all these things impact each other. But all of it needs to be coordinated if you're going to come out with the best result.

There's a brain that sits atop your anatomical structure for a good reason. It's so that your body can coordinate all the many processes your body undertakes, often at the same time. Just picking up a glass to take a drink of water could be a disaster if your brain weren't calling the shots. You have to reach for the glass, lift it carefully, position your face, open your mouth, and then swallow the water without choking on it. It doesn't seem like much because your brain's neurons and your muscles work so well together. But these are complex tasks. In everything we do, there are multiple processes, neurons firing, muscles being dispatched to action, counter-balancing movements from other parts of the body—your brain quarterbacks all of it.

Your investment guy or gal is going to be very good at moving stocks around, buying and selling, to get the best return. But are they tied into your tax situation? Do they know where you are with all the other elements of your financial picture, to keep the IRS at bay in your life?

It's important to make sure your team is working together.

It's important to know all your team players are specialists in their individual fields.

And it's important to be certain they have your best interests in mind.

It's an area we work on at our firm. Communication is key. We try to make available the best in-house team that can be offered. We can't help our client effectively if we're not able to pull all these aspects together to work in concert for the best long-term results for our client. And we're always trying to improve. I've mentioned a goal of bringing in a travel agent, for example.

You wouldn't expect to find someone like that in our kind of business, but we love helping people in every way we can. If a client has had a dream of an overseas trip, we want to show how that's possible financially, and then we want to help him or her make those plans without ever leaving the building. You'd be amazed how much pleasure we derive from little things like that. It's where the real fun comes in for us.

We're always trying to improve our teamwork.

TOWARD A WONDERFUL FUTURE

We've talked a good bit about money. That's the subject that caused you to open this book. It's the number one source of anxiety for most of us. Your desire is to know how your money will best help you in a future of retirement.

But here's the goal: to think about money as little as possible. Money is much more enjoyable when we don't have to be concerned with it. We want our clients to have the good time, the life-culminating party, that they've waited many years for. If you're someone who has worked for decades to reach this moment, you certainly don't want a future of feverishly watching your investments and wondering whether you've over- or under-budgeted.

This time is supposed to be all about *you*—you, the people you love, and the activities you love. Money is just the way we take care of those things in our culture. So as you seek the best guidance in financial planning for retirement, remember your goal is to create a plan, and that plan will do the work that allows you to have the fun.

If we can help you do that, we'd love to hear from you. You can contact us through our website www.fiatwm.com. But even if that's not the case, we want to wish you the happiest retirement, the fulfillment of all your dreams, and a continued prosperity that will create a legacy for your children and for the world around you.

You may be on the way down the mountain, but that's really just another way of saying a new adventure is beginning. Enjoy the party!

ACKNOWLEDGMENTS

MY JOURNEY IN THE FINANCIAL INDUSTRY HAS BEEN A LONG one. I started from scratch, with no formal education in this arena. Luckily, I've met many wonderful people along the way, who invested their time and energy in me both personally and professionally. They helped to make every page of this book possible.

To my business partner and friend, Matt Stahl: I have a lot of crazy in me, and you've always put up with me and found a way to level me out. Fiat is what it is because of you.

To Tom Wade and Ryan Poterack: Your mentorship over the years has directly impacted my life and a lot of the pages of this book, so much so that you deserve to be mentioned by name.

To the hundreds of other financial advisors I've met over the years: You were willing to share your stories, ideas, and education to help make me a better advisor to the families I serve. You all know who you are. If you're sitting there thinking, "Is he talking about me?" the answer is probably yes!

GRAPHICS SOURCES

GRAPHIC 1:

Sources: BlackRock; Informa Investment Solutions. This graphic looks at the effect that the amount withdrawn from a portfolio has on how long that portfolio may last. A prudent withdrawal rate (3% to 5%, adjusted and revisited annually) can increase the probability of success. Other factors that may affect the longevity of assets include the investment mix, taxes, expenses related to investing and the number of years of retirement funding (life expectancy). This is a hypothetical illustration starting at the beginning of a severe stock downturn in 1973 to 1974. Beginning withdrawals in a rising market could improve the longevity of your portfolio. The portfolio is made up of 50% stocks and 50% bonds. Stocks are represented by the S&P 500 Index, which is an unmanaged group of securities and considered to be representative of the stock market in general. Bonds are represented by the Barclays Government Bond Index, which is an unmanaged index comprised of all publicly issued, non-convertible debt of the US government, its agencies of quasi-federal corporations and corporate or foreign debt guaranteed by the US government. Inflation is represented by the Consumer Price Index. This illustration assumes a hypothetical initial portfolio balance of $1,000,000 as of December 31, 1972, and monthly withdrawals beginning in 1973. Each monthly withdrawal is adjusted annually for inflation. Each portfolio is rebalanced monthly. All dividends and interest are reinvested. Results will vary based on selection of other time frames and over time as assumptions change. These figures are for

illustrative purposes only and do not represent any particular investment, nor do they reflect any investment fees or expenses, or taxes.
It is not possible to invest directly in an index. Past performance is
no guarantee of future results.

GRAPHIC 2:

https://www.irs.gov/retirement-plans/plan-participant-employee/
retirement-topics-required-minimum-distributions-rmds

GRAPHIC 3:

https://www.ssa.gov/planners/taxes.html

GRAPHIC 4:

None

GRAPHIC 5:

Source: BlackRock. This graphic looks at the effect the sequence
of returns can have on your portfolio value over a long period of
time. Other factors that may affect the longevity of assets include
the investment mix, taxes and expenses related to investing. This is
a hypothetical illustration. This illustration assumes a hypothetical
initial portfolio balance of $1,000,000 with no additions or with-
drawals and the hypothetical sequence of returns noted in the table.

These figures are for illustrative purposes only and do not represent any particular investment, nor do they reflect any investment fees, expenses, or taxes.

GRAPHIC 6:

Source: BlackRock. This graphic looks at the effect the sequence of returns can have on your portfolio value over a long period of time. Other factors that may affect the longevity of assets include the investment mix, taxes and expenses related to investing and the number of years of retirement funding (life expectancy). This is a hypothetical illustration. This illustration assumes a hypothetical initial portfolio balance of $1,000,000, annual withdrawals of $?0,000 adjusted annually by 3% for inflation and the hypothetical sequence of returns noted in the table. These figures are for illustrative purposes only and do not represent any particular investment, nor do they reflect any investment fees, expenses, or taxes. When you are withdrawing money from a portfolio, your results can be affected by the sequence of returns even when average returns remain the same, due to the compounding effect on the annual account balances and account withdrawals.

GRAPHIC 7:

None

GRAPHIC 8:

Sources: BlackRock. The projections shown above assume the withdrawal in the first year of the state percent of the original portfolio value. Each year thereafter, the amount withdrawn is adjust upward 3% to account for inflation. IMPORTANT: The projections or other information generated by BlackRock regarding the likelihood of various investment outcomes are hypothetical in nature, do no reflect actual investment results and are not guarantees of future results. A probabilistic approach is used to determine the likelihood that you may be able to achieve the goal of the stated withdrawal rate. Probabilistic (Monte Carlo) modeling is a statistical modeling technique in which a set of future outcomes is forecasted based on the variability or randomness associated with historical occurrences. It involves generating thousands of scenarios, each simulating the growth of assets over a specified period of time, taking into account a variety of factors, such as economic conditions, the allocation of assets, portfolio value, net cash flow and market volatility. This analysis is not a guarantee, prediction or projection of any particular result and your actual results may vary materially. Rather, this analysis is directional in nature and can be used to help you evaluate how certain decisions or strategies may impact your ability to achieve your goals. Underlying each scenario presented in this analysis are certain capital market assumptions (e.g., rates of return, volatility as measured by standard deviation, correlation between asset classes). These are forward-looking rates of return developed by BlackRock. The capital market assumptions regarding rates of return for various asset classes and the probability analysis applied to these returns are key to the underlying results. In this analysis, stocks have an expected return of 7.25% and a standard deviation of 17% while bonds have an expected return of 3% and a standard deviation of 4.5%. Other investments not considered may have characteristics similar or superior to those being analyzed. There is no guarantee that actual future market returns will be consistent with these assumptions and limitations.

ABOUT THE AUTHOR

BRAD GOTTO, RETIREMENT INCOME CERTIFIED PROFESSIONAL (RICP), founded Fiat Wealth Management in 2009 to help clients align their money with their personal beliefs. He uniquely applies techniques in behavioral finance, investigation, and mathematics to unlock personal freedom. Host of the podcast, *Every Day is Saturday*, Brad provides financial education workshops for families free of charge throughout the Twin Cities, where he lives with his wife, Christy, their two sons, William and Hudson, and their Golden Retriever, Kinnick. For more information, visit www.fiatwm.com.

Made in the USA
Monee, IL
17 October 2023